The Art of Frank Norris, Storyteller

the art of

Frank Norris, Storyteller

Barbara Hochman

University of Missouri Press
Columbia, 1988

University of Missouri Press, Columbia, Missouri 65211
Printed and bound in the United States of America

Library of Congress Cataloging-in-Publication Data

Hochman, Barbara.
The art of Frank Norris, storyteller.

Bibliography: p.
Includes index.
1. Norris, Frank, 1870–1902—Criticism and interpretation. 2. Self in literature. I. Title.
PS2473.H6 1988 813'.4 87-19201
ISBN 0-8262-0663-8 (alk. paper)

∞™ This paper meets the minimum requirements of the American National Standard for Permanence of Paper for Printed Library Materials, Z39.48, 1984.

To my mother and my father

Preface

This book began as an effort to come to terms with the strengths and anomalies in Frank Norris's work and a wish to clarify the grounds of my own stubborn interest in a writer whose initial popularity had long since been replaced by the apathy of both scholars and readers. Norris's contemporaries knew how to value his gifts; William Dean Howells rated him above any other writer in his generation. But in the decades following Norris's death at the age of thirty, only isolated voices continued to speak for his originality, his seriousness, his humor.

During the last fifteen years, there has been a sustained and concerted effort to revise Norris's status as a curiosity and as a representative of that anachronistic literary mode "naturalism." Since the 1970s, a great deal of fresh criticism has appeared. A comprehensive bibliography, a new edition of Norris's letters, and several new editions of his major novels indicate an upsurge of interest in Norris. In 1980 Don Graham's collection of new essays (like his earlier book-length study) revealed, as he had hoped, a "multi-faceted Norris, not the naive naturalist too often presented in the past" (Introduction to *Critical Essays on Frank Norris* 1980, xii). Yet Graham's words are still true today: no one has "defined the essential Frank Norris" (xvii).

My own contribution to the effort of definition approaches Norris's fiction on the basis of recurrent motifs that resist incorporation into the pattern of meanings traditionally attributed to his work. I believe that the Norris to emerge from this particular reading is one that will bring us closer to the intense, vital, creative spirit so well loved by friends, family, and public in his own time, and only recently glimpsed again in ours.

Acknowledgments

I would like to thank a number of people for their help in the course of my work on Norris. Kenneth M. Dauber's comments on the logic and implications of my argument were always apt and provocative. Joshua Wilner helped clarify my thinking on *The Octopus* at a crucial moment. John Landau offered astute advice at several other critical junctures. Marcus Klein and Joseph R. McElrath, Jr., read the completed manuscript with care and were generous with cogent responses. Shlomith Rimmon-Kenan, with her characteristic incisiveness, helped me articulate some narratological points. Glen Love and Richard Alan Davison made valuable comments for final revisions. Baruch Hochman's intellectual rigor and moral support were invaluable throughout.

I am also grateful to the students who, in the beginning, alerted me to the loose ends of *McTeague*. And my thanks to *Studies in American Fiction* and *Western American Literature* for permission to reprint earlier versions of the chapters on *McTeague* and *Vandover*.

B.H.
January 1988

Contents

1. Norris's Dubious Naturalism

> "You don't understand. . . . It runs in my family to hate anything sticky. It's—it's—it's heredity."
>
> —Annixter in Norris's *The Octopus*

> So you think Romance would stop in the front parlor and discuss medicated flannels and mineral waters with the ladies? Not for more than five minutes. . . . She would find a heart-ache (may-be) between the pillows of the mistress's bed, and a memory carefully secreted in the master's deedbox.
>
> —Norris, "A Plea for Romantic Fiction"

This study grows out of the conviction that the imaginative force of Frank Norris's work is not to be sought in his naturalist concerns, but rather in a cluster of preoccupations that center on the vulnerability of the self. Norris's fiction generates an image of the self in perpetual engagement with life processes beyond its control, struggling for a measure of equilibrium within the relentless flow of internal and external pressures. Although desperately in search of control and order, the individual is seen to be easily thwarted, virtually helpless under stress, afraid of change, loss, and human contact. Nonetheless, Norris's vision increasingly allows for the possibility of constructive responses to experience. Unexpectedly, and unobtrusively, his work comes to affirm the stabilizing power of memory, language, and art.

The image of a potentially vital, though also precarious, self emerges from the dialogue, events, and imagery of Norris's fiction; it cannot be derived from the ideological formulations of the narrative voice. Since the naturalistic thrust of the fiction receives essential support from its discursive passages, however, a sharp contradiction emerges. Not only do the "naturalistic" formulations within the novels often fail to provide a meaningful framework for the central imaginative cruxes of the text, but the philosophical passages even deflect attention from the more subtle and compelling implications of the dramatic structure. Perhaps the readers who made Norris's work so popular in its day were responding to something other than the overt naturalistic themes that were later increasingly hailed as the defining characteristic of his work.[1]

On the surface, Norris's fiction certainly looks like exemplary "literary naturalism." The pattern of events and the rhetoric of the narrative voice are typical of the tradition. Norris's first two major novels, *Vandover and the Brute* and *McTeague,*[2] plainly enact the pattern of individual passivity, degeneration, and destruction exemplified by the protagonists of such naturalistic texts as Zola's *L'Assommoir,* Dreiser's *Sister Carrie,* or Stephen Crane's *Maggie: A Girl of the Streets.* The main characters of both *Vandover* and *McTeague* undergo a radical decline in fortune after a period of stability and even contentment. McTeague's physiognomy at once recalls Zola's Laurent *(Thérèse Raquin)*[3] and reflects Caesare Lombroso's ideas about the criminal personality-type. Vandover's submission to the disease that turns him into a virtual beast—barking like a wolf and crawling on all fours—is analogous to McTeague's reversion under stress first to his own earlier way of life, as depicted at the start of the novel, then to his father's alcoholism and brutality, and finally to a condition in which he displays the sixth sense of the hunted animal.

Indeed, the progressively declining fortunes depicted in Norris's first novels neatly illustrate various aspects of the theories of heredity, reversion, and atavism popular in his day. The interpretive comments of the narrative voice further amplify these notions. Vandover's "fatal adaptability," like that of Gervaise in *L'Assommoir,* is repeatedly emphasized, while in *McTeague* the "omniscient" narrator tends to stress the inexplicable influence of heredity, instinct, chance, and combinations of circumstances beyond the control of the characters.

Given such blatantly "naturalistic" emphases, it is hardly surprising that for over half a century Norris's fiction was considered unadulterated "American literary naturalism."[4] Only in the last twenty years have a number of critics reexamined the relative standing of Norris's ideas within his work. Donald Pizer's initial—and seminal—study of the novels viewed Norris's philosophical ideas as sustained and consistent. In a later essay, however, Pizer himself reassessed a passage of typical social Darwinism within *Vandover and the Brute* and concluded that its ideas, rather than accounting for Vandover's fall, serve to reflect the hero's state of mind.[5] As Don Graham states in the introduction to his fine study of Norris's work, "Social Darwinism is an image for Vandover's fear; it is important, not as a belief, but because it reveals how Vandover thinks: in the clichés of his age."[6]

The work of Pizer, Graham, McElrath, and others has challenged the assumption that Norris's fiction can be adequately accommodated within the naturalist rubric. Yet it remains supremely difficult to achieve a stable perspective on Norris's philosophical ideas. Even the passage analyzed by Pizer and Graham remains ambiguous when seen in the context of similar passages elsewhere in *Vandover.* Cast in almost identical language, these recurrent evocations of individual submission to the "resistless," "relentless," forces of "Nature" serve different functions in relation to different characters and events.[7] Characteristically, the text fails to sustain a consistent perspective on the Darwinian ideas scattered throughout. While these ideas sometimes appear to be a measure of Vandover's inability to think for himself or, elsewhere, a measure of Geary's self-interest, they are nonetheless often indistinguishable from the pronouncements of an "omniscient" narrator, apparently articulated with the blessings of the author himself.

There is no getting around the fact that the naturalistic formulations in Norris's fiction sometimes remain irreducibly ambiguous. The final lines of *The Octopus* provide the most notorious example of such ambiguity. Despite the destruction of life and spirit that Presley has witnessed in the course of the novel, the narrative voice tells us that he has been converted at last to the "larger view" of life—the conviction that "the Truth . . . will, in the end, prevail, and all things, surely, inevitably, resistlessly work together for good" (II, 361). While in principle evolutionary idealism may incorporate rather than contradict other aspects of a naturalist vision, many readers of *The Octopus* have taken the meliorism of its closing lines as an evasion, not a resolution. The persistent debate over interpretation of this passage is itself a measure of the difficulty.[8] Evaluation of the text's concluding "optimism" depends on the question of whether *The Octopus* as a whole supports or subverts Presley's final perspective. This question would be unanswerable even if we could clearly distinguish—as we cannot do—between Presley's final opinions and those of the narrative voice.

Moreover, even when theoretical formulations within Norris's work are unambiguously affirmed by the narrator, they shed very little light on the implications of the dramatic action and often threaten the imaginative vitality and structural coherence of the text. An extreme example will typify the problem. In *McTeague,* two references to the notion of inherited traits provide the only theoretical or naturalistic "explanation" for the transformation of Trina Sieppe from a trim model of housewifely virtue into the ravaged, obsessive miser who is finally murdered by her husband.

Trina's transformation, one of the most powerful sequences in Norris's fiction, is not adequately explained by reference to her "penurious" ancestors or her roots in a "hearty mountain race." The occasional references to her "instinct of hoarding" or the power of Chance do not go much further in clarifying her destruction either. The many essays that have grappled with the logic of Trina's undoing testify to the gap within *McTeague* between the theoretical formulations in the text and the events they would seem to interpret.[9] This gap is present throughout Norris's work.

Trina's deterioration, like the experiences of Norris's other protagonists, can be most clearly elucidated by focusing on the non-ideological thrust of the fiction and, particularly, on the imaginative coherence implicit in its events, dialogue, and imagery. This coherence—the focus of the present study—can be fully revealed only after the texts' explicit ideological statements are provisionally set aside. Indeed, the amount of emphasis that has been placed upon Norris's "philosophy" is somewhat bewildering, especially given the limited scope and cogency of philosophical ideas within the texts themselves. It is hardly surprising, for example, that the naturalistic case for Trina's degeneration fails to persuade readers when it is based on the narrator's blatant and limiting formulas. In both *The Octopus* and *The Pit,* moreover, the discursive passages seem at once increasingly difficult to attribute to an "authoritative" narrator and increasingly hard to apply in relation to the action.

Norris's typically naturalistic plots, his grim, "scientific" descriptions, and Darwinian rhetoric remain stubbornly difficult to reconcile with other aspects of his work. Norris's critical writing, and his juvenilia and personal correspondence further complicate the issue. Despite his fascination with naturalistic doctrine, Norris himself always tends to undercut his literary affinities, even as he affirms them. In "Zola as a Romantic Writer," an essay Norris wrote while working on *McTeague,* he mentions seven novels by Zola but "[c]uriously enough," as Åhnebrink puts it, he fails to mention *L'Assommoir,* "a novel which influenced him greatly at this time" (111). Norris's omission of *L'Assommoir* in such a context may be taken as a sign of the complexity involved in establishing his most meaningful literary sources and affinities. Norris's ironic reference to himself as "the boy Zola"—a phrase with which he often signed letters and inscribed frontispieces—only underscores the ambiguities of his relationship to his ostensible model.

In his critical essays, Norris defines *naturalism* as the antithesis of "realism" and the ally of "romance." Such an eclectic emphasis amplifies, and in turn is further amplified by, tensions within his own fiction. As Don Graham points out, "[b]y perceiving Zola as a romantic writer [Norris] effectively scrambled . . . traditional categories" to such an extent that it becomes impossible to say just what Norris's work is a "textbook" example of.[10]

Furthermore, despite the intermittent statements of philosophical naturalism to be found within his fiction, Norris himself leaned, temperamentally, neither to science nor to philosophy.[11] Though his letters often dealt with his own writing—with the progress of his work, his particular plans, hopes, and ideas—his correspondence is singularly free of philosophical thrust. There is just as little philosophical substance in his critical essays.

A comment by Norris in "The Novel with a Purpose" seems illuminating in this context: "Do you think that Mrs. Stowe was more interested in the slave question than she was in the writing of *Uncle Tom's Cabin*?" Norris asks.

> Her book, her manuscript, the page-to-page progress of the narrative, were more absorbing to her than all the Negroes that were ever whipped or sold. Had it not been so, that great purpose-novel would never have succeeded. (92)

Though Norris's statement may shed little light on *Uncle Tom's Cabin,* it seems a meaningful gloss on his own relation to "ideas" in fiction. To Norris, presumably, the "page-to-page progress of the narrative" was far more compelling than theories of heredity, determinism, or the "irresistible forces of nature." The present study will reflect on the meaning and function, for Norris, not only of "naturalism" but of writing and narrative, as such.

Long before Norris was a "naturalist," he was a writer—a storyteller, poet, correspondent, keeper of notebooks and diaries. His complex relation to both narrative per se and "naturalistic" narrative deserves more critical attention than it has received. Norris clearly valued scientific data, for example, taking copious notes on dentistry, lycanthropy, criminal personality, atavism, and so forth. Yet even at the level of explicit formulation, Norris was essentially committed to the aesthetic effect of truth, rather than to scientific or philosophical demonstration: "'It's not the things that have really happened that make good fiction,'" says a writer named Strelitz in Norris's short story "His Sister," "'but the things that read as though they had'" (*Frank Norris of the Wave,* 34). Norris affirms the same view in his critical writings.[12] He repeatedly draws a distinction between surface accuracy on the one hand, and "truth" on the other. In "A Plea for Romantic Fiction," he makes his well-known charge that "Realism" notes "only the surface of things" (76). For Norris, fidelity to factual details—accuracy as such—is not a primary value in fiction. Norris's own attention to research and documentation functions partly in the service of what he calls accuracy, not truth, but his bid for the former is surely not intended to be at the expense of the latter.[13]

Norris spoke of naturalism as a synthesis of literary modes that would be equal to the task of representing "the unplumbed depths of the human heart" and the "unsearched penetralia of the soul of man"

("Plea for Romantic Fiction," 78). Don Graham persuasively shows that Norris in fact challenged realism "on its home ground," using the "objective decor" of American interiors ("surface accuracy") as a "base" for his attack. Graham speaks of Norris's novels as an attempt to "combine explorations into the 'black, unsearched penetralia of the soul of man' with commonplace detail, bisque statuettes, and the like." The "bisque statuette," as Graham shows, repeatedly makes its way into both Norris's fiction and criticism; yet the implications of the image and its function have not been exhausted. In "A Plea for Romantic Fiction," a bisque fisher boy appears not only as a measure of realism's "tameness and limitations" but also to suggest one term of a dialectical process repeatedly dramatized in Norris's work.[14]

Norris claims that Realism "stultifies itself" with its attention to surfaces. It is Romance, he insists, that is "equally at home in the brownstone house on the corner and in the office building downtown," Romance that can penetrate the surface it contemplates ("A Plea for Romantic Fiction," 77). Norris anticipates his reader's negative reaction to these views:

> But would you take [Romance] across the street to your neighbor's front parlor (with the bisque fisher boy on the mantel and the photograph of Niagara Falls on glass hanging in the front window); would you introduce her there? Not you. . . . No indeed. . . . You just guess you would not.
>
> She would be out of place, you say, inappropriate. She might be awkward in my neighbor's front parlor, and knock over the little bisque fisher boy. Well, she might. If she did, you might find underneath the base of the statuette, hidden away, tucked away—what? God knows. But something which would be a complete revelation of my neighbor's secretest life. ("Plea for Romantic Fiction," 76–77)

The bisque statuette is certainly part of a style Norris rejects, a measure of Gilded-Age triviality. But it is also one of many objects, artifacts, and activities that Norris's protagonists depend upon to satisfy a common need: the need to contain the "turbulence" that, in Pizer's formulation, is always just "beneath the [commonplace] surface" of life within the fictional world of literary naturalism in general, and within Norris's work in particular.[15]

In Norris's fiction the relationship between commonplace surface and subterranean turmoil is not merely one of polarity, either in the external world or within the self. Rather, like the relationship between the bisque statuette and the neighbor's "secretest life," all the commonplace habits and accoutrements of life in society are seen to be part of a continuous, dialectical effort through which the self, embodied in one character after another, struggles for a measure of equilibrium within the chaos of experience. The depiction of this process in its various forms and with various results is a central emphasis in Norris's work. Both Norris's relationship to naturalism, and his vocation as a writer, can be illuminated in relation to this process.

Among the diverse weapons used by Norris's characters in their struggles for stability are the constructs of philosophical naturalism themselves. The notion of survival of the fittest helps Vandover to amplify his fears and yet rationalize his failure, while Geary (like Moran or Shelgrim in *The Octopus*) freely invokes Darwinian categories in support of his own self-interest.[16] Presley, thrashing around in search of a position that might enable him to tolerate the brutal reality he lives in, alternately embraces Caraher's political radicalism, Shelgrim's view of "Force," and Vanamee's evolutionary "optimism." For individual characters (as perhaps for Norris himself), naturalistic formulations sometimes appear, almost magically, to possess a reassuring, order-making power. But when the same language serves such a variety of purposes in the experience of his characters, Norris's naturalism cannot provide a stable perspective for the reader.

The imaginative coherence of Norris's work may therefore be said to derive not primarily from his philosophical ideas but from his keen intuition about dynamic processes through which the individual self strives to make peace with the unstable external conditions of existence on the one hand and the insoluble "mystery" of the human heart on the other. Throughout Norris's fiction both unreliable external reality and unstable inner reality are presented as "givens," inextricably woven into the nature of things. Moreover, Norris's work increasingly affirms the need to accept rather than to fight the flux, process, and mystery that his fiction presents as the basic condition of life.

Norris's fiction never presumes to "solve" the mysteries of the human condition by applying philosophic truths or scientific knowledge. Norris apparently felt, quite as much as Hawthorne or James, that, in narrative at least, the truth "of the human heart" was not to be arrived at either through documentation or through philosophical argument. In fact, the scientific-philosophical quest, far from appearing to provide a solution to the problems of either art or life, is a direct target of Norris's irony from the start of his career.

An early sketch in the form of a "Platonic dialogue" among five toys in a playroom dramatizes the futility and the absurdity of pursuing "the truth" about man's relation to God and/or nature. "The Puppets and the Puppy," a parody of philosophical discourse, was first published in *The Wave* during Norris's second year as a regular contributor.[17] The sketch thus appears before the publication of any of Norris's major fiction, but after the considerable work he had done on both *Vandover* and *McTeague* while studying creative writing at Harvard in 1894–1895. The sketch provides a paradigm for a number of elements in Norris's later work. Not only does "The Puppets and the Puppy" parody the notion of scientific or philosophical certainty, it does so using a range of phrases that reappear intermittently throughout Norris's fiction.

In the course of "The Puppets and the Puppy," the five toys (a chess piece, a lead soldier, a doll, a mechanical rabbit, and a wooden manikin from a Noah's Ark) discuss the logic and conditions of their existence in "The Room." They debate the existence of "The Boy," "a certain Force that moves us from time to time—a certain vague power, not ourselves, that shifts us here and there" (176). They consider the extent of their own freedom, and the Queen's Bishop says that even the "Force" that moves them can do so only "along certain lines." The Doll mocks the chess piece's certainty of the existence of a "Force," agreeing with the lead soldier and the mechanical rabbit that there is a boy who moves the toys about, winds them up, and occasionally throws them away.

In the course of the discussion, various speakers invoke the notion of the gradual "betterment of the race," the inscrutably "vast, grand scheme of the Room," and "the vast, grand plan of events" (178). The toys assume that although these ideas cannot be verified, "there must be reason in them" (179). Just as the lead soldier is holding forth about the role of "Accident," a fox-terrier puppy comes into the playroom and destroys the entire cast of characters. The Queen's Bishop is the last to disappear, "muttering, vaguely, something about the vast, resistless forces of nature" (180).

The absurdity of "The Puppets and the Puppy" is derived from the reader's inevitable awareness of the "true" state of things. I have been suggesting that one of the most difficult problems facing a reader of Norris's work is that of interpreting the thrust of the discursive formulations in the text, whether those of the protagonist or those of the narrative voice. Many of Norris's readers have become uncomfortably aware that his fiction generally fails to illuminate the nature of the "forces" repeatedly said to be at work within the represented world. The reader of *Vandover and the Brute* or *The Octopus* remains as ignorant of the nature and meaning of these forces as Norris's benighted protagonist himself.

In the case of "The Puppets and the Puppy," however, such obstacles to interpretation are much less formidable. Here the reader has a wider perspective than the characters themselves, and that wider perspective provides understanding that, up to a point, is clearly distinguishable from the blindness of the Queen's Bishop and his fellow "puppets." Unlike the characters in the dialogue, the reader cannot be deceived about the existence of The Boy, the nature of "the lines" along which the chess piece believes its movement to be restricted, the existence of the Puppy, and the absence of any "vast, grand plan of events" for "the betterment of the race." With obvious metaphoric thrust, the sketch suggests that human beings are woefully deceived about the most basic conditions of their own lives.

The epigraph to "The Puppets and the Puppy" is a quotation from *Hamlet,* with a twist: "There are more things in your philosophy than are dreamed of in Heaven and Earth." As a forerunner of the dialogue, these lines underscore the irony directed at the notion of meaningful philosophical discourse. Each of the characters displays a mixture of foolishness, pomposity, earnestness, and reasonable accuracy. Among the more perceptive characters is the Doll, with its apt inference that "there is a Boy and I am made in his image." The Doll is contemptuous of the Queen's Bishop, with his emphasis on the forces of Nature: "'You think you've solved it all—you with your science and your learning,'" says the Doll.

The Doll's skepticism about scientific truths would seem to express one of Norris's own attitudes. Yet the Doll is nonetheless capable of pretentious theoretical discourse, no less than the Queen's Bishop. Thus, the dialogue seems to imply that while our quest for "truth" is inevitable and its motivating force far from mean or reprehensible, the end so devoutly to be wished can never be achieved. Seen in this light, the sketch is at once a parody of sophistry and a dramatization of the futile—if irrepressible—human wish for the comfort of clarity and meaning.

The language and structure of the dialogue have additional implications. In "The Puppets and the Puppy" the terms used to suggest such typical naturalistic cruxes as free will versus determinism, the nature of force, or the teleology of existence are terms that recur with striking regularity throughout Norris's fiction. The dialogue ends, for example, by invoking the very formula repeatedly cited both in *Vandover and the Brute* (by Geary, by Vandover, and by the narrative voice) and in *The Octopus* (1901). If the notion of "the vast, resistless forces of nature" is ironically undercut in "The Puppets," one cannot automatically assume that Norris invested the same phrase with solemn meaning in works that both precede and follow the sketch by several years. The function of Norris's naturalistic phraseology varies, not only from work to work but also within individual novels, depending on the context.

More revealing than the language of "The Puppets and the Puppy," however, is the structure of this sketch, which follows a pattern that is typical of Norris's later work. From *McTeague,* published two years after "The Puppets," through Norris's last novel, *The Pit,* published in 1903, a sudden, unexpected event serves as a climax of the action. While sudden catastrophe is a familiar element of literary naturalism in general, its effect within Norris's work is manifold. In "The Puppets" the unexpected aggression of the Puppy dramatizes the limits of individual power or freedom, while making a mockery of the effort to establish "philosophical" or "scientific" certainty. Nevertheless, as the sudden upheaval itself reveals, the "puppets" in the dialogue are not entirely wrong; they are not totally deluded. They simply dwell in what Keats called "a state of half-knowledge." And the sketch implies that there is absolutely no way for them—or us—to move from half-knowledge to certainty.

Within Norris's vision, the willingness to eschew the "quest for certitude" emerges as a cardinal value.[18] Unlike Zola, who hopes for the eventual discovery of "laws" by which to explain human behavior, and unlike Dreiser, whose work intermittently expresses guarded optimism about our gradually increasing insight into human nature, Norris's work speaks ever more strongly for the need to renounce the very impulse toward definite knowledge and control. Moreover, that renunciation is itself seen as a source of strength and a ground for hope.

Another formulation by Keats seems oddly illuminating in this context and directly applicable not only to "The Puppets" but to a major concern throughout Norris's work. I refer to the letter in which Keats coins the phrase, "Negative Capability," the faculty that he sees as the indispensable quality of a literary man. It is the quality that, according to Keats, "Shakespeare possessed so enormously."

> I mean Negative Capability, that is, when a man is capable of being in uncertainties, mysteries, doubts, without any irritable reaching after fact and reason . . . of remaining content with half-knowledge.[19]

In "Novelists of the Future," Norris writes that the proper training of the novelist is the "achieving less of an aggressive faculty of research, than of an attitude of mind—a receptivity, an acute sensitiveness" (13). Norris's pejorative sense of the "aggressive faculty of research" closely resembles Keats's rejection of the "irritable reaching after fact and reason." At the same time, the growing emphasis within Norris's work on the value of "receptivity" suggests that Norris comes to see the capacity of "remaining content with half-knowledge" as an increasingly valuable asset in a world where certainty cannot be achieved at any price.

Whether or not Norris was well-acquainted with Keats's correspondence, a juxtaposition of the two writers illuminates Norris's literary and intellectual affinities.[20] Norris sees a basic opposition in life between the capacity to remain "content with half-knowledge" on the one hand, and the "irritable reaching after fact" on the other—or, as Keats puts it in another letter, the opposition between "those who delight in Sensation" and those who "hunger . . . after Truth."[21]

Many of Norris's views, concerning both literature and the nature of things, crystallize around this particular set of issues. Norris's often-stated sense of opposition between "life" and "literature" involves an explicit dichotomy between "the heart" and "the head," between feeling and knowledge.[22] The implications of this dichotomy lead to the notion of multiple polarities: between energy and form, fluidity and fixity, imagination and stultification, child and man. All of these contrasts, including the last, play a vital role in Norris's conception of both life and art.[23]

Norris's distinction between "accuracy" and "truth" evolves along similar lines. "To be true is the all-important business," Norris writes in "A Problem in Fiction." "Paint the horse pea-green, if it suits your purpose" (58). Far from being the result of science and research or philosophic argument, then, truth is born of spontaneity, receptivity, intuition and imagination. Moreover, for Norris, it is precisely the capacity for imaginative truth that distinguishes men from "puppets."

From Norris's point of view, the inaccessibility of objective truth is not ultimately a cause for despair. Altogether, Norris's work (like his personality), far from exhibiting rage or grief at lack of certainty, displays a growing optimism. The movement from *Vandover and the Brute* or *McTeague* through *The Octopus* and *The Pit* involves an increasingly direct confrontation with the complexities of the self and a turning away from the fear and grimness that color Norris's early work. The source of the optimism is more personal than cosmic, however.[24] It is a belief in the value of personal relationships and inner sources of strength (including imagination and consciousness). This belief is grounded in a recognition that all relationships are provisional, as are all strength, all happiness and, indeed, all life.[25] Such a point of view, barely implicit in Norris's early work, receives its fullest expression in *The Octopus* and *The Pit*.

For Norris, in life, the antidote to fear or despondency, isolation and uncertainty, was not philosophical distance or scientific knowledge, but human contact and artistic productivity. Within his work, Norris's most constructive resolutions involve the recognition that while man's lack of clear knowledge or control is inevitable, life is nonetheless worth living. In Norris's earliest fiction, such recognition is well beyond the capacity of the characters themselves. Indeed, Norris's first protagonists merely respond to a world of incomprehensible pressures with a range of desperate efforts to make some kind of order out of the chaos of inner impulses, and the flux of external conditions. This wish to make order and to seize control is seen from two perspectives. Norris's first novels, especially, include comic figures, like Trina's father, or Old Grannis and Miss Baker, whose efforts to establish order and dominate either the inner or the outer world sometimes end with a whimper and a bang. However, these characters coexist with more abysmal failures—characters who are subject to mounting terror and desperation as the action unfolds.

In *McTeague,* the Sieppe family, especially Trina's father, provides a comic paradigm for man's failure to impose order on himself or his surroundings. The Sieppe episodes hinge on Papa Sieppe's need for order and his tendency to contribute to disorder, both propensities reaching their peak during the preparations for Trina's marriage. Trina's father relies on his organizational rigor to ward off the acute discomfort that, for him, attends virtually all activity and certainly all change.

The Sieppe family's passion for order merely provides a comic analogue to the preoccupations of the novel's major characters, all of whom are engaged in ineffectual efforts at controlling their environment and containing inner turmoil. Trina's hoarding of gold, McTeague's collection of invariable habits, Maria Macapa's obsessively repeated story, even Old Grannis's bookbinding—all of these repetitive occupations constitute desperate efforts to impose one's will upon the flow of one's experience, one's instinctual needs, or one's disconcertingly unstable surroundings.

Such measures tend to proliferate within the world of Norris's fiction, often in response to somewhat mysterious or unspecific threats. Both Vandover, Norris's first fictional protagonist, and Jadwin, his last, suffer physical torture from an ailment with no specific cause.[26] Uncontrollable inner processes and external events of unknown origin consistently provoke the greatest fear to which Norris's characters are subject. Vandover repeatedly experiences the "catastrophes" that overtake him as the unexpected "springing of . . . successive mines beneath his feet" (*Vandover and the Brute,* 437). The letter from City Hall banning McTeague from practicing dentistry is "like a clap of thunder" (*McTeague,* 193). In *The Octopus* nothing elicits the characters' fear and rage more consistently than the sudden appearance of S. Behrman, the ineluctable railroad representative who repeatedly refuses to specify his demands or name his terms.[27] Altogether, Norris's characters, like the characters of Zola, Hardy, Crane, and Dreiser, live in a world where they are repeatedly rendered impotent and desperate by unforeseen circumstances, chance events, and forces that seem to be driving them relentlessly to their destruction.

Yet despite the treacherousness and instability of life as depicted in Norris's work, his fiction contains at least the emergent possibility of creating meaning in consciousness and within human relationships. In *Vandover* and *McTeague,* defensive maneuvers and obsessive behavior constitute typical efforts to deal with the treacherous conditions of life. Norris's subsequent work (beginning with *Blix,* 1899) explores other, more benign and life-giving responses to existence in a world where there is little to rely on and plenty to fear.

Norris's work increasingly depicts a process through which the individual struggles for some sense of meaning and self-consolidation. The vision of such a process, and the renunciation of the quest for certitude, implies a conception of experience and of the self that sometimes more clearly reveals Norris's romantic rather than his "naturalist" heritage.[28] At the same time, Norris's choice of weapons in the struggle for "identity" or equilibrium points to the governing issues of early modernist fiction, with its emphasis on aesthetic form and the inner life. Norris's work ultimately affirms memory, consciousness, imagination, and art as the potential grounds of salvation for the tenuous self.

A recurrent motif in Norris's fiction is the effort to create a feeling of order and stability through a structure made of words. In *Van-*

dover and the Brute (1899), Bancroft Ellis compulsively keeps a notebook of facts and figures to which he regularly turns at times of doubt or stress. In *McTeague* (1899), Maria Macapa repeats a phrase and a story. In *Blix* (1899), Condy and Blix read and write fiction; the old diver and Captain Jack spin "yarns," while KDB learns the encyclopedia by heart. In *A Man's Woman* (1900), Ward Bennett keeps a meticulous journal in the face of approaching death. All of these activities are variants of the effort to combat the horrors of powerlessness by objectifying and fixing experience in language and form. "How terrible death must have seemed before it had been given a name," a character reflects in Norris's early story "Lauth" (1893, 130). Perhaps even Norris, keeper of notebooks,[29] and writer of fiction, was himself engaged in a process of mastering terror through the word.

By any calculation, Norris produced all his major fiction within five years. Nevertheless, striking changes of both method and meaning are evident. In the "early" fiction (*Vandover* and *McTeague*), Ellis's reliance on his notebook of facts and figures and the Sieppe family's compulsive organizational frenzies constitute typical defensive responses to the ebb and flow of life. As Norris's fiction develops, however, such strategies are replaced by more searching, often artistic responses. Ward Bennett's journal in *A Man's Woman* provides a convenient paradigm for this shift. Don Graham, one of Norris's most perceptive critics, calls *A Man's Woman* "obsessive in denying any value to art or intellectual activities, such as thinking, talking and writing."[30] Still, Bennett's journal plays a considerable role within the text. Beginning as a purely objective record of names, dates, places, dwindling provisions, and deaths, it later becomes the basis for Bennett's discursive story of his Arctic expedition. Bennett's book is written only after the survivors of the expedition are rescued and after the death of his best friend Ferriss. Indeed, partly because Bennett's own behavior contributes to Ferriss's death, the book he later writes becomes a "labor of love" for Ferriss (*A Man's Woman,* 241).

A Man's Woman is universally regarded as Norris's weakest novel; it fluctuates between the grotesque and the sentimental. Yet it provides a rich schematic exemplification of Norris's central concerns, including the concern with narrative structures. Throughout Norris's early work, vulnerable characters create a sense of safety for themselves through mechanical repetition, often cast in language. In Norris's later novels a contrast emerges between automatistic, deadening repetition and another kind of repetition, one that opens up the possibility of integrating experience. After *McTeague,* embracing the future increasingly impels Norris's characters to confront the past in order to avoid literally reenacting certain aspects of it, interminably reliving it in memory, or compulsively repeating it as story. It is as if Norris intuited the healing power that Freud, his elder contemporary, was beginning to find in benign reconstruction of life-narratives as a way of undoing the compulsive reenactment of early trauma and loss.

In *A Man's Woman* Ward Bennett undergoes a transformation from aggression and defiance to humility and love. During a crucial stage of this process, Bennett—ill and delirious—relives the events of his recent past. The scene of Bennett's delirium suggests a mode of memory, or of reliving the past, that involves a realignment of its components, thereby increasing rather than constricting the possibilities of life. "'Where's Ferriss? Where's Richard Ferriss? Where's the chief engineer of the Freja Arctic Expedition?'" Bennett calls feverishly (219). "Rapidly and in a low voice he began calling off the muster of the Freja's men and officers, giving the answers himself" (219). Bennett responds "here" after every name he calls, until he gets to that of Ferriss. He calls for Ferriss repeatedly, but receives no answer. Finally, he begins again,

> calling to mind a different order of things: "Adler—here; Blair—died from exhaustion at Point Kane; Dahl—here; Fishbaugh—starved to death on the march to Kolyuchin Bay; Hawes—died of arctic fever at Cape Kammeni; McPherson—unable to keep up, and abandoned at ninth camp; Muck Tu—here; Woodward—died from starvation at twelfth camp; Dr. Sheridan Dennison—frozen to death at Kolyuchin Bay; Chief Engineer Richard Ferriss—died by the act of his best friend, Captain Ward Bennett!" Again and again Bennett repeated this phrase, calling: "Richard Ferriss! Richard Ferriss!" and immediately adding in a broken voice: "Died by the act of his best friend, Captain Ward Bennett." (219–20)

Bennett at once relives and rewrites his own history in this sequence; Ferriss had died only *after* his safe return home, and under circumstances within which Bennett, at the time, had played a brutally aggressive role, quite without compunction. Bennett's revision of both the facts themselves and his view of those facts leads to the inner transformation that facilitates his marriage, and to the period of creativity during which he writes the story of his arctic adventure. Thus, it may not be surprising that after *A Man's Woman,* Norris's work increasingly explores both the possibility of individual change through the integration of recollected experience and the problems that arise from fixation upon a particular segment of the past.

The running soliloquy in which Bennett reinterprets his recent experience constitutes one of the few moving passages in an extremely bizarre book. It is, indeed, only a temporary reprieve. Bennett, at the end of the novel, resumes his struggle to dominate the "Enemy" outside. It becomes his intention once again to subdue Nature and the elements of ice and snow.[31] At the end of *A Man's Woman,* as at the start, Bennett is determined to conquer the Unknown, man's greatest enemy throughout Norris's fiction, here embodied in vast uncharted Arctic regions. Beyond this, Bennett, like his sublimely supportive wife, the indomitably brave nurse, means to challenge Death itself.

In Norris's best work, such goals are repeatedly undercut. Norris's major novels are grounded in the recognition that one cannot conquer nature, death, or time, can never achieve permanent happiness or certain truth. In *The Octopus* (1901) and *The Pit* (1903), value is seen to reside precisely in the willingness to accept these limits, limits inherent in the human condition. Annixter of *The Octopus* provides the best example of a character who comes to recognize the inevitability of process, yet who nonetheless comes to affirm life and even to risk himself in human relationships. Annixter renounces both the need to dominate others and the need to barricade himself within a system of defensive isolation. Although he himself creates neither narratives nor any kind of art, Annixter does confront his experience in memory and consciousness. Like Ward Bennett, Annixter is said to have "wrought out his salvation" (II, 94) one night by confronting his recent past and "coming, at last, to himself" (II, 102).

Memory, art and verbal structures, whether oral or written, are related components of Norris's vision. With increasing directness his work confronts both the positive and the negative aspects of memory, language, and art. The storytelling habit in particular is seen alternately as a constructive and a destructive factor in the process of assimilating experience into a self that is resilient enough to bear the unstable conditions of existence.

In this context it seems oddly fitting that before Norris himself began writing narratives, he trained for a life as a painter. Within Norris's work, the depiction of stultified characters gradually gives way to a focus on characters who grapple with the need to accept flux, rather than dominate it. Perhaps this movement is analogous to Norris's own shift from the frozen, spatial images of visual art to the time-art of narrative. Norris's changeover from the medium of paint to the medium of words (and subsequently from poetry to prose) may have foreshadowed his novels' increasing concern with the need to accept a still more fluid medium: life itself. Norris's own route to the acceptance of flux was love and friendship, imagination and art. Gradually he mapped out an analogous route for his characters. One vital aspect of the process rendered in Norris's fiction is the dynamic of narrative itself. The idea of storytelling takes many different forms within Norris's work. It is a concept that deserves independent consideration as a prelude to detailed analysis of the major novels.

2. *The Power of the Word*

> . . . the *story,* as a mere story, is to the story writer the one great object of attention.
>
> —Norris, "The Novel with a 'Purpose'"

Throughout his fiction, articles, and personal letters, Frank Norris incorrigibly referred to novels as "yarns." "Tell your yarn and let your style go to the devil," he said and wrote at every opportunity; "we don't want literature, we want life."[1] Norris's assiduously cultivated yarn-spinner image has seemed of a piece with his rejection of aestheticism and his emphasis on "virile fiction." The repeated critical and biographical references to Norris as a "born story-teller," a "story-teller by instinct," however, do not begin to explain the special and complex meaning that storytelling had for Norris.[2]

Franklin Walker's still standard biography takes as its starting point Norris's image of the storytelling child within the man. "Within the heart of every mature human being, not a writer of fiction," Norris wrote in "Story-Tellers vs. Novelists," "there is the withered remains of a little story-teller who died very young." Norris elaborates this idea at some length.

> Every healthy-minded child—no matter if he develops in later years to be financier or boot-maker—is a story-teller. As soon as he begins to talk he tells stories. . . . And the love of good fiction and the appreciation of a fine novel in the man of the world of riper years is—I like to think—a sort of memorial tribute which he pays to his little dead playmate of so very long ago. (65–66)

The link suggested here between storytelling, memory, and death is not fortuitous; it recurs in a variety of forms throughout Norris's fiction and critical writings. It is this cluster of issues, rather than Norris's own early death, that gives the notion of the "little story-teller who died very young" a special relevance to Norris's work.

From *Vandover and the Brute* through *The Pit* Norris's fiction is pervaded by a concern for the means by which the vulnerable self struggles for balance within the vagaries of experience. Beset by capricious impulses from within, subject to myriad pressures from without, characters in Norris's fictional world generate a variety of stabilizing mechanisms. In one recurrent strategy, narrative structure (like other kinds of aesthetic form) functions as an antidote to internal and external flux. Throughout Norris's work, characters repeatedly find that reading, writing, or telling stories affords them at least a temporary sense of order or control, some measure of inner equilibrium.

Within Norris's fiction, certain modes of storytelling stultify the self, while others foster human contact or individual growth. For certain characters, the repetition of a story becomes an adaptive mechanism through which the memory of a particular past experience serves to fortify (or sometimes petrify) the self against the pressures of the present. Other characters read and reread stories for similarly defensive purposes. Confining themselves to a limited selection of literary texts, these figures turn from the unpredictability of inner and outer reality to the reliability of language, aesthetically composed. Still others—more vital, courageous, or richly faceted characters—make a more dynamic use of stories, whether produced or consumed.

The most constructive relation to narrative within Norris's work involves either literally writing fiction (so long as "life" is not excluded in the process), or constructing a version of one's own experience that facilitates one's relation to the present without defensively stultifying the self. The character who achieves such a perspective on the events of his recent (or not-so-recent) past need not elaborate it into a full-blown narrative; the vision can be crystallized within a moment of consciousness. Nonetheless, such ordering can facilitate a character's movement through time and space, enabling him to risk contact with others, to release spontaneous feeling, and even to acknowledge the painful inevitability of change and death. Thus, Norris sees the spontaneous storytelling child within the man as potentially valuable for everyone, not only for the writer of fiction.

The facts of Norris's own storytelling history would seem to inform his view of narrative. Certainly Norris retained a vivid sense of the storytelling child he considered himself to have been. The storytelling aspect of Norris's relationship with his brother is well documented. Like the Brontë children, who sustained a lifelong involvement with the fabled world that sprang from their box of wooden soldiers, the Norris boys extended the imagined lives of their lead soldiers well beyond childhood. The lead soldiers made their way into Norris's adolescent writing and into the mature work of both Charles and Frank. In fact, Norris's last novel, *The Pit,* is dedicated to his brother,

> in memory of certain lamentable tales of the round (dining-room) table heroes; of the epic of the pewter platoons, and the romance-cycle of "Gaston le Fox," which we invented, maintained, and found marvelous at a time when we both were boys.[3]

We have few particulars about Norris's storytelling relationship with his fiancée largely because Norris and Jeannette Black burned their correspondence after their marriage. Still, we know that Norris placed a high value on his wife's opinion of his work and on her literary judgment in general. Certainly the relationship between Condy and Blix, in Norris's most nearly autobiographical novel, is pervaded by stories read, heard, and written together. Perhaps similar experiences bonded the Norrises as well.

Given the centrality of storytelling both to Norris's life and to the life of his fiction, it is surprising how little notice has been taken of the numerous stories—read, heard, told, and written—that appear within his work. Norris's characters go to the opera and to vaudeville shows, look at paintings good and bad, play concertinas and pianos, but most of all they read and tell stories. Condy and Blix read Kipling; Presley reads Homer; Annixter reads and rereads *David Copperfield*; Annie Derrick immures herself within the work of Tennyson and Walter Pater; Jadwin loves *The Rise of Silas Lapham*; Page and Landry Court devour a great and motley assortment of fiction. Virtually every novel Norris wrote contains diaries, notebooks, journals, or works of literature that are depended on, worried over, and in the process of being produced. But even more regularly, characters struggle with the story of their own experience. Obsessive storytelling provides many of Norris's characters with the means to impose some kind of order—often highly rigid order—upon events, especially events of the past. Maria Macapa in *McTeague,* the old diver in *Blix,* Dyke and Caraher in *The Octopus,* and for a time Ward Bennett in *A Man's Woman* compulsively retell stories of loss.

It is usually the obsessive minor characters who make narratives directly out of the stuff of their personal experience; the professional writers (and other artists) in Norris's fiction do not use their own experience as material for their work. Still it is not only the compulsive peripheral characters who use storytelling and other aesthetic forms to organize their experience and to impose some kind of coherence on the self.

An incident from *Blix* provides a convenient paradigm for some of these issues. Blix and Condy's love for one another begins on the day they listen to the strange story told by an old ship's mate aboard a wheat ship to which they have been drawn in pursuit of journalistic material for Condy. The ship's mate tells the couple how, as a young diver, he had been sent to recover the dead body of a nineteen-year-old girl who had drowned off the coast of Ceylon. "'I'll have to tell you,'" the mate explains to Blix and Condy,

> "that when a body don't come to the surface it will stand or sit in a perfectly natural position until a current or movement of the water around touches it. When that happens—well, you'd say the body was alive; and old divers have a superstition—no, it *ain't* just a superstition, I believe it's so—that drowned people really don't die till they come to the surface, and the air touches them. . . . When I went down the second time . . . [t]here was the girl. . . . Her eyes were wide open, and she was looking right at me and smiling. It didn't seem terrible or ghastly in the least. She seemed very sweet. . . .
>
> ". . . The next thing to do was to send her up. But I began to think. . . . If I left her there she'd always be sweet and pretty—always be nineteen; and I remembered what old divers said about drowned people living just so long as they stayed below. . . . Well, I signalled to be hauled up. They asked me . . . if I'd seen anything and I said no. . . . They never raised the ship, and in a little while it was all forgotten.
>
> "But I never forgot it, and I always remembered her. . . . And I've growed to be an old man remembering her; but she's always stayed just as

> she was the first day I saw her. . . . She's always stayed young and fresh and pretty. . . . Somehow I never could care for other women after that, and I ain't never married for that reason." (133–34)

Both Condy and Blix are enchanted by this story. "'Fine, fine; oh, fine as gold!'" Condy murmurs, and Blix "gravely" raises a wine glass with a toast "to *her*" (134). Their enthusiasm over "the *story* of it!" (136) endures for quite some time, becoming part of the bond between them and the ground of a sustained effort on Condy's part to write a story of his own, which he calls "A Victory over Death."

However, Blix and Condy's enthusiasm for the shipmate's story—"'Isn't it a ripper! Isn't it a corker!'" (136)—does not begin to exhaust the possible resonance of the tale within Norris's work. Several other perspectives are provided within *Blix* itself. The mate's tale is preceded, for example, by his apparent doubt as to whether to tell it at all. "'I dunno,' he said, pulling his beard, 'I don't usually tell that story to strange folk; but you remind me so of her [he says to Blix] that I guess I will'" (132). Despite this apparent reluctance, it soon turns out that the ancient mariner of *Blix*—like Coleridge's Ancient Mariner—is in fact in the habit of retelling his story regularly. On the way off the ship, Condy and Blix meet the captain of the whaleback who asks if they got what they wanted from "old McPherson."

> "More, more!" exclaimed Condy.
>
> "My hand in the fire, he told you that yarn about the girl who was drowned off Trincomalee. Of course, I knew it. The old boy's wits are turned on that subject. He *will* have it that the body hasn't decomposed in all this time. Good seaman enough, and a first-class navigator, but he's soft in that one spot." (135)

The captain's denigration of McPherson makes no impact on Condy and Blix, but it should alert the reader to the compulsive aspect of the old man's tale. McPherson is only one in a long line of storytellers whose ubiquitous presence within Norris's work is the more striking for having gone unnoticed.

From *McTeague*'s Maria Macapa, through Caraher, Vanamee, and Dyke of *The Octopus,* to Old Hargus of *The Pit,* Norris's work proliferates characters whose entire emotional lives are fixed upon a devastating moment of experience in the past. Most of these characters rarely miss a chance to tell their story and, as in the case of McPherson, the storytelling generally serves to deflect the potentially disturbing impact of past events. Frequently the storytelling becomes a substitute for ongoing present experience. McPherson believes that the girl in the sea has remained unchanged for fifty years, though the captain denies it; surely he himself appears to have changed very little. The narrative voice in *The Octopus* says of Vanamee that his "life had suddenly stopped at a certain moment of its development" (I, 32). The same could be said of the ship's mate who has never married and who has (to the best of his ability) eschewed immersion in ordinary life processes. Though we cannot say of McPherson (as the narrative voice does of both Vanamee in *The Octopus* and Corthell in *The Pit*) that the passing of years has had virtually no effect on his physical appearance, it is clear that whatever the young McPherson's feelings might have been when he found a beautiful girl at the bottom of the sea, the story he has created out of the experience is not a source of pain or grief for the old ship's mate. As in Ariel's song in *The Tempest* ("Full fathom five thy father lies; / Of his bones are coral made; / Those are pearls that were his eyes" I.2.400–401), the verbal composition replaces death and loss with an image of beauty and some kind of form.[4]

We could say of McPherson's story and his relationship with the dead girl, as of the figures on Keats's Grecian urn, "never, never canst thou kiss / . . . yet, do not grieve / . . . . For ever wilt thou love, and she be fair" ("Ode on a Grecian Urn," lines 17–20). The connection is not a fanciful one. Indeed, it points the way to an imaginative crux not only of *Blix* but of all Norris's work.

The diver's experience is a paradigm for what Condy and Blix must avoid at all costs. The sacrifice of ongoing life on the altar of "perfection" is one of Norris's specific targets when he raises his battle cry of "life" rather than "literature." (Within his fiction, Corthell of *The Pit* provides the best example of such stultification.) Although *Blix* is often spoken of as an "idyll," it is also a rejection of idylls. At the end of the novel, Blix and Condy make a choice and an affirmation rarely achieved by characters in Norris's work, many of whom stand at analogous crossroads. Despite their fears, Condy and Blix decisively reject the possibility of parting from one another, with their own perfect "idyll" enshrined in memory. They decide instead to expose it to "reality," to the pressures of commonplace daily life, to movement through time and space.

When the last chapter of *Blix* begins, Condy and Blix have acknowledged their love for one another and are reveling in it, despite their awareness that Blix is to leave Condy the next day for her studies in the East.

> That New Year's Day was to be the end of everything. Blix was going; she and Condy would never see each other again. The thought of marriage—with its certain responsibilities, its duties, its gravity, its vague troublous seriousness, its inevitable disappointments—was even a little distasteful to them. Their romance had hitherto been without a flaw. . . . It was as well that it should end that day, in all its pristine sweetness, unsullied by a . . . single disillusion or disappointment. Whatever chanced to them in later years, they could at least cherish this one memory of a pure, unselfish affection. (271–72)

Just as Blix is saying "'so long as we love each other, *time* won't matter'" (276), Condy discovers in his pocket the sealed letter from the Centennial Publishing Company. He opens it and reads aloud their invitation to him to become assistant editor of their East Coast *Quarterly*.

What the lovers "said then, they could never afterward remember" (277), but the result is a decision to stay together and the words themselves cease to matter. The commitment to a fixed and idealized memorial image has in effect been transformed into a readiness to risk moving ahead with life. And appropriately enough, no sooner do they choose to embark on their future than they find themselves already "beyond the confines of the garden" (278), with their "innocence" behind them:

> It was the end of their gay, irresponsible, hour-to-hour life of the past three months; and it was the beginning of a new life, whose possibilities of sorrow and of trouble, of pleasure and of happiness, were greater than aught they had yet experienced. They knew this—they felt it instinctively, as with a common impulse they turned and looked back upon the glowing earth and sea and sky . . . —all that scene that to their eyes stood for the dear,

> free, careless companionship of those last few months. Their new-found happiness was not without its sadness already. (277)

Condy and Blix, at the end of the novel, prove unique within Norris's fiction in their willingness to move ahead into the unknown future with full recognition that life is not likely to be perfect, and yet without the need either to embalm or to reject the past entirely.

In this sense, the lovers prefigure a value conceptualized with increasing subtlety and clarity in Norris's later works: the value of synthesizing and integrating experience, including the experience of loss, into a self that is resilient enough to move forward with experience while sustaining a sense of the past. It proves a difficult goal to achieve. Many of Norris's characters seem to live only in the past; others would repudiate the past altogether. When Laura and Jadwin, at the end of *The Pit,* leave their old home to go West, Laura refuses even to take a final look at her old house, despite Jadwin's suggestion that she do so. Her intention is to think only of the "new life," which she insists will be without a flaw. It is as if to look back would be to risk turning into stone. So incapable is Laura of connecting her past to her future that she cannot even allow herself a parting glance.[5]

Although characters within Norris's work rarely rise to the challenge of integrating experience, the challenge continues to present itself. Indeed, most of Norris's protagonists face dangers, both internal and external, far more threatening then those encountered by Condy and Blix, or even Laura and Jadwin. Vandover moves from fear and desperation to humiliation and indifference. McTeague robs, kills, and flees to Death Valley; Trina becomes an obsessive miser, a mutilated woman, and finally a victim of murder. Instances abound in which the self is all but desperate for a stable haven—even a refuge like the diver's—as protection against flux, uncertainty, and loss. Characters regularly seek such refuge through memory, through art, through a repeated narrative, or through other obsessive behavior that seems to arrest the movement of time and relieve the pressure of internal and external stress.

The pattern changes from novel to novel, but in one form or another, it is present in them all. Thus, Norris's first novel, *Vandover and the Brute,* dramatizes not only the way Vandover, a talented painter, fails to be "saved" by his art (as he hopes) but also the way memory and verbal discourse fail to serve as constructive forces for the integration of experience. Vandover's view of his own experience, indeed, makes him the antithesis of the diver in *Blix*. "It was always a matter of wonder to Vandover," the novel begins, "that he was able to recall so little of his past life."

> With the exception of the most recent events he could remember nothing connectedly. What he at first imagined to be the story of his life, on closer inspection turned out to be but a few disconnected incidents that his memory had preserved with the greatest capriciousness, absolutely independent of their importance. (281)

The attentive reader soon comes to mistrust Vandover's judgment as to whether his particular memories are significant or trivial. But the novel as a whole certainly bears out Vandover's sense of his own failure to impose imaginative coherence upon "the story of his life."

Vandover's experience as presented in the novel involves an increasingly desperate effort to respond constructively to catastrophe and loss. Though Van begins as an aspiring painter, his art finally degenerates into lines with "no meaning" (477), as do the lines he speaks. Vandover's failure gains added metaphoric resonance by virtue of the degenerative disease to which he is subject. Because of his lycanthropy, Vandover eventually barks and growls like a wolf; he can no longer rely on his ability to speak at all. Toward the end of the novel Vandover loses even his capacity to remember "recent events . . . connectedly." This loss is most sharply dramatized when a disheveled and incoherent Vandover appears before his old, now rich and successful friend Geary:

> "I'm no good!" [Van] said at length, wagging his head and blinking through his tears. "I'm—I'm done for and I ain't got no money; yet, of course, you see I don't mean no offence. What I want, you see, is to be a man and not give in and not let the wolf get me, and then I'll go back to Paris. Everything goes round here, very slow, and seems far off; that's why I can't get along, and I'm that hungry that sometimes I twitch all over. I'm down. I ain't got another cent of money. . . . I had to sell [my] bonds—had some debts you see, my board and my tailor's bill. They got out some sort

> of paper after me. Yes, I had forgotten about my bonds. I lost every damned one of them playing cards." (570)

As Geary listens, mostly silent and incredulous, Vandover produces a second and then a third version of how he lost his bonds. His singularly lengthy narrative finally ends as follows:

> "But I'd be all right if everything didn't go round very slowly, and seem far off. But I'm a wolf. You look out for me; best take care I don't bite you! Wolf—wolf! Ah! It's up four flights at the end of the hall, very dark, eight thousand dollars in a green cloth sack, and lots of lights a-burning. See how long my finger nails are—regular claws; that's the wolf, the brute! Why can't I talk in my mouth instead of in my throat! That's the devil of it. When you paint on steel and iron your colors don't dry out true; all the yellows turn green. But it would'a'been all straight if they hadn't fined me! I never talked to anybody—that was *my* business wasn't it? And when all those eight thousand little lights begin to burn red, why, of course that makes you nervous! So I have to drink a great deal of water and chew butcher's paper. That fools him and he thinks he's eating. Just so as I can lay quiet in the Plaza when the sun is out. . . . Oh I don't complain. Give me a dollar and I'll bark for you." (572–73)

This soliloquy is only the most eloquent testimony to Vandover's final, fatal inability to make sense out of the "story of his life." His colors no longer "dry out true"; he can't "talk in his mouth"; in fact, as he puts it, "I never talked to anybody." As his efforts to paint on canvas degenerate into lines with "no meaning," so his effort to tell Geary about his recent past is self-contradictory and increasingly incoherent.

Though Vandover's story, as told to Geary, is strangely moving, its lack of simple *narrative* coherence—its failure as the telling of a sequence of events—makes it the diametrical opposite of the shipmate's tale in *Blix*. And perhaps it is no accident that Vandover degenerates physically and emotionally, just as his language degenerates, while the diver lives to a ripe old age, telling his story to anyone who will listen.

The protective mechanism of the diver in *Blix* has much in common with that of Maria Macapa, the primitive maid-of-all-work in *McTeague*. More elaborately than *Vandover, McTeague* dramatizes a considerable range of inadequate responses to the ebb and flow of life, failed efforts to use language and art as stabilizing structures in a dangerously fluid world. In *McTeague,* Maria Macapa, like the old diver, repeatedly narrates a story of loss. Again like the diver, Maria at the start of the novel is relatively untouched by the pressures of time and insulated from the stresses of intimate contact with others. She seems to be relatively safe—at least as long as she goes on telling her tale. Her sudden amnesia with regard to her story leads directly to her death.

Maria's "yarn" is the antithesis of Vandover's fluid and self-contradictory narrative. Her story is more than coherent; it is eloquent. And it is not merely formed; it is so fixed and formulated as to be easily repeatable. Indeed, Zerkow, who basically marries her for her story, eventually learns it by heart.

McTeague himself, unlike Maria, is sublimely inarticulate. Although his concertina may be said to provide some outlet for expression, McTeague's musical expressiveness is limited to six tunes played over and over again and one song whose lines are cited and repeated in the text. Thus, like Maria's narrative and Trina's interminable whittling of miniature Noah's arks, the very form of the aesthetic medium would seem to serve a function that is defensive rather than expressive.[6] Usually, the content of the aesthetic object—song, story, or painting—provides a further gloss on the nature of the threat being contained through formal means. In Trina's case, for example, the tiny toys she produces are literally bulwarks against the chaos of flood waters.

Norris's last two novels subtly complicate and reexamine the governing concerns of the early fiction. *The Octopus* and *The Pit* are Norris's most ambitious works; *The Octopus* is in many respects his finest. *Vandover and the Brute* and *McTeague* present a vision of the failed and desperate efforts—mostly defensive ploys—through which individuals struggle to ward off the dangers that surround them from without and threaten to subvert them from within. The vision of the self within both *The Octopus* and *The Pit* suggests a wider range of possibilities. Although both novels present characters almost as stultified as Maria Macapa or the sea-diver, they also depict characters who venture to divest themselves of their defenses.

Annixter is perhaps the most successful as well as the best known of Norris's heroes, who, in the course of his rendered experience, sheds his protective armor and adopts a posture of receptivity. This change is accomplished largely in the course of Annixter's all-night vigil, from which he emerges with a new perspective on a series of recent experiences. With the help of his altered perspective on the past, a new future seems to open before him. That future turns out to be much shorter than Annixter could have anticipated; indeed, Norris has been accused of killing Annixter because "he could take him no further."[7] One could speculate that in the case of Moran, too, Norris was unable to envision the next step in the process for the self that renounces its defensive posture, embraces change, and exposes itself to intimate human contact. Yet Annixter's death, like Moran's, exemplifies a serious, if obvious, issue. Like Achilles, the man or woman who acts spontaneously upon rage or love, without regard for self-defense, becomes extremely vulnerable.

Annixter's importance within *The Octopus,* however, goes beyond his increasing receptivity to experience and to others, beyond his increasing vulnerability and sudden death. Norris's portrait of Annixter is also his most positive projection of the qualities that sustain the creative imagination.

At first glance, *The Octopus* is certainly not a book about art or poetry, despite the presence of Presley and his large literary ambitions. Presley is trying to write an epic when the novel begins, but he cannot find "his inspiration." Though determined to write his "Song of the West," he feels that he was born too late. "Reality was what he longed for, things that he had seen. Yet how to make this compatible with romance?" (I, 20). The West that Presley sees in his imagination—his "great scheme of harmony"—keeps coming up against "immovable facts" (I, 10). Then the "romance" becomes "realism, grim, unlovely, unyielding" (I, 10). Presley, unlike Norris, does not know that "romance" is not to be found by resisting "immovable facts" or by rising above them, but by recognizing them in their full relation to the deeper reality they often conceal, as "the little bisque fisher boy" in the "neighbor's front parlor" may conceal, "underneath the base of the statuette, hidden away, tucked away . . . a complete revelation of my neighbor's secretest life" ("Plea for Romantic Fiction," 77).

Unlike Norris, Presley cannot find a place within his "frontier of Romance" (I, 7) for the "uncouth brutes of farmhands and petty ranchers, grimed with the soil" (I, 3), who populate the San Joaquin Valley, as he knows it. Presley wants to write of "a new race, a new people . . . primitive, brutal, honest, and without fear" (I, 7). He seeks to capture "their lusts, their blunt, grim humor, their stoicism under stress" (I, 7), but all he encounters is the "eternal fierce bickerings between the farmers of the San Joaquin and the Pacific and Southwestern Railroad [which] irritated him and wearied him. . . . It was material, sordid, deadly commonplace" (I, 10).

Presley cannot integrate his discordant impressions within his own consciousness, nor can he synthesize them within a work of art. Yet the pattern of allusions and events in the first chapter of *The Octopus* suggests that the capacity for such integration is crucial, not only to art but to the life of a vital, experiencing self.

In the first episode of the novel, Presley arduously makes his way to the top of a little hill where, although he comes closer to grasping his inspiration than ever before, his "Song of the West" remains well beyond his grasp. Don Graham has convincingly analyzed this scene in terms of Mallarmé's "Late Afternoon of a Faun."[8] Other poetic analogues come to mind. Presley, smoking lazily on his little hilltop, becomes "drowsy": "By degrees, the sense of his own personality became blunted, the little wheels and cogs of thought moved slower and slower. . . . A delightful numbness invaded his mind and his body" (I, 41–42).

Presley's state here recalls the "drowsy numbness" of the speaker in Keats's "Ode to a Nightingale"; his dissociated consciousness suggests the lack of "self" found in Keats's "chamelion poet." Alternatively, Presley may be seen to resemble Wordsworth's "wise passiveness" or Emerson's transcendentalist, transformed through contemplation of nature into a "transparent eyeball," saying, "I am nothing; I see all."

Regardless of the specific analogues, a sharp critique of Presley emerges. Presley can perceive or record certain things, but he himself indeed is "nothing." He may fail to execute his "Song of the West"; he does not even attempt a "Song of Myself." Like Mallarmé's or Emerson's speaker, like Keats's nightingale poet, Presley would inhabit a realm above the earth, transcending everyday limitations. But unlike the nightingale poet, he does not make the return trip to his "sole self." When Presley's "idyl" is interrupted by the slaughter of Vanamee's sheep at the end of Chapter I, his reaction, typically, is to turn away with revulsion, just as he flees America at the end of the novel.

Thus, Presley, "a poet by training," avoids both "reality" and himself, escaping from "immovable facts" into romance. His friend Vanamee, "a poet by instinct," does something similar by adhering with stubborn tenacity to an idyl of his own. Vanamee's heart is said to be "in the little coffin in the Mission garden" (I, 36). Like the diver in *Blix,* Vanamee "never forgot" (I, 33) his dead beloved, his lost image of perfect bliss. His conviction at the end of the novel that he has come to prove "Time was naught; change was naught. . . . Death was overcome" (II, 106) involves a mad belief that he has literally transcended "immovable facts"—to live an idyl, if not to write one.

The third young hero of *The Octopus* would not seem to believe in idylls. Furthermore, he is not a poet; he is a "man's man," gruff and tough, suspicious of virtually everyone and everything, despite an inordinate "respect [for] the man who could rhyme words" (I, 24). Annixter certainly does not consider himself an artist, nor is he presented as one; yet, like Presley and Vanamee, he too has a "vision" in the presence of newly sprouting wheat.

I have intimated that Annixter's vision (unlike theirs) involves a confrontation with his innermost self—his own needs and wishes, the role he has played in his relationship with others. More interesting, however, is the fact that Annixter's "vision"—his recognition of his love for Hilma Tree—is cast in the same terms as Presley's problem writing his "Song": in terms of the imagination that synthesizes. Sitting on his own little hill, "a great white stone [that] jutted from the ground" (II, 78), Annixter sees the woman he loves as "an ever-present reality," "a tangible imminent fact," and sees the idea of marriage as a "formless far-distant abstraction." Then slowly, Annixter's "imagination . . . be[gins] to work." He begins to "think less and feel more." He gives "his imagination full play," and soon "things as disassociated in his mind as fire and water [are] . . . fused together." A "little seed at first weak, forgotten, lost in the lower dark places of his character" begins to germinate (II, 80–82).[9]

The image of a natural, growing plant, an organic whole, is a familiar romantic image for the work of art. The notion of the synthesizing imagination is equally familiar. Within Norris's frame of reference, only an imagination that, unlike Presley's, can fuse "things as disassociated . . . as fire and water" can hope to produce either a work of art or a self resilient enough to entertain contradictions, perhaps even to "contain multitudes." Such an imagination, apprehending the inextricable interrelatedness of joy and sadness, ugliness and beauty, even life and death, is seen as one that can potentially accept the vagaries of the inner life, as well as the outrages of external reality. Norris placed a high premium on such an imagination and the life-affirming self that generates it.

Norris's fiction is crowded with evocations of arrested development, characters whose paralysis provides a sharp contrast with "organic" being, whether of the individual or the work of art. In Norris's early work, characters repeat stories mechanically and obsessive behavior abounds. In his later work obsessive mourners, failed artists, and compulsive storytellers coexist with characters whose lives suggest the possibility, if not the actual reality, of integrating ongoing and often contradictory experience. Moreover, such experience is depicted in a context increasingly dense with images of flux and natural process.

If a positive vision—not an idyllic one—emerges from *The Octopus* and *The Pit,* it is a vision whose corollary may be found in Norris's notion that the mature talented writer sustains the storytelling instinct of the child, an instinct that does not die but, on the contrary, grows in strength. Norris's emphasis in "Storytellers vs. Novelists," and elsewhere, on the value to the writer of preserving the child he once was, confirms the implication of the fiction that "the child is father of the man," in life as well as literature. In Norris's critical writing, the death of the spontaneous, storytelling child is a serious loss that cannot be redeemed by any power of thought or intellect. Force of will or mind is not enough to produce good fiction without the "auxiliary of the little playmate of the old days" ("Storytellers vs. Novelists," 68).

This "little playmate of the old days" is linked in spirit to the writer's indispensable "attitude of mind" that Norris describes in "Novelists of the Future." No "handbook" or "textbook," Norris insists, can help the writer of fiction who has lost his capacity for "receptivity" or for what Norris, like Keats, calls "watchful[ness]" (13).[10] Norris's reflections on the creative imagination, scattered throughout his critical essays, not only contain echoes of many terms used by Keats, they also suggest Wordsworth's conception of the child who comes to earth "trailing clouds of glory," only to be slowly deadened by the "walls of the prison house" that progressively close in upon him.

In "Novelists to Order—While You Wait" Norris, though explicitly rejecting the notion of "God-given" genius, speaks of the "original 'spark' in the child mind" (14) that tends to be eventually extinguished. Unlike Wordsworth, Norris sees the creative imagination threatened not merely by the nature of civilization per se; he attacks the particular trend of American society in his own time: "No one ever heard of obstacles thrown in the way of the boy who announces for himself a money-making career," Norris writes,

> while for the artist . . . education, environment, the trend of civilization are not merely indifferent, but openly hostile and inimical. One hears only of those men who surmount—and at what cost to their artistic powers—these obstacles. How many thousands are there who succumb unrecorded!
>
> . . . when you have choked the powers of imagination and observation, and killed off the creative ability, and deadened the interest in life, don't call it lack of genius. (15–17)

Norris repeatedly suggests that preservation of the "original 'spark' in the child mind," like preservation of the child's erstwhile storytelling instinct, is absolutely essential to a writer of fiction. Moreover, Norris's novels dramatize a similar value in life as well: the value of maintaining some access to one's childhood, to a past self that is neither apotheosized nor left behind and forgotten, but that may be drawn upon as life proceeds. Norris's fiction moves from images of the failure to do so, to images of possible success, sustaining the child, one's past self, and integrating it into one's present field of experience.

In *The Pit,* Norris's last novel, Laura is confronted by a problem that plagues characters throughout Norris's work. Beginning with Vandover, characters intermittently conceive of themselves as an uneasy alliance, or as a battleground, of multiple selves. Laura repeatedly experiences a sense of being "two Lauras," but her conflict is most sharply dramatized through her recurrent sense of despair over the loss, not of a treasure or a dead love but of the self she used to be. Her recurrent grief over the "little black-haired girl of Barrington" she once was is the measure of her inability to integrate her former self or selves into a present being capable of growth and change—or at least one whose present form she can live with in peace.

It does not seem improbable that Norris's work on *The Pit* took him back to aspects of his own childhood.[11] Not only did Norris dedicate *The Pit* to his brother in memory of "the knights of the round (dining room) table," the setting of *The Pit* is Chicago, where Norris spent his childhood until age fourteen. The city of his birth is one whose claim upon him Norris apparently rejected with a vengeance once his family moved to California. Franklin Walker suggests that Condy's statement, "'Bawn and rais' in Chicago, but I couldn't help that you know,'" summed up Norris's feelings as well (*Letters,* viii). In fact, when asked by a reviewer for biographical information following the favorable reception of *Moran,* Norris eliminated all reference to the role of Chicago in his past. "I was bawn 'n raise' in California," Norris wrote to Marcosson (*Letters,* 23).

"There are [only] certain cities in the world that are adaptable to the uses of the writer of fiction," Norris wrote in "An Opening for Novelists" (28). With most of his fiction set in California, Norris's praise of San Francisco is hardly surprising: "Consider [the story-value of] San Francisco," Norris writes. "It is not necessary to hesitate a moment." On the other hand, he comments derisively, "no romancer has yet had the hardihood to attempt to write of Chicago or Buffalo. Imagine a novel of Chicago!" (28–29). In light of these opinions, it is worth pondering Norris's choice of Chicago as the scene for his last novel—and especially when one reads *The Pit* as a study of multiple selves and the challenge of integrating experience, a story of memory and growth.

Many of Norris's friends and acquaintances, as well as various students of his work, have felt that shortly before he died Norris was on the brink of a new creative departure. Joseph McElrath in his "Biographical Essay" suggests that "Norris seems to have been beginning a change of perspective and life-style" by 1902. "Hard facts are admittedly scarce and speculative gestures are a consequence," McElrath writes. "Much seems to have been going on at the end."[12] Indeed, we do not know why Norris canceled his plan to travel around the world, or why he changed the projected title of his last, never-to-be-written volume of the wheat trilogy. Neither can we explain—we can but note—Norris's having achieved a level of intimacy with his brother that, according to the latter, they "never before [had] reached."[13]

Within the confines of Norris's work, of course, the changes are easier to identify. Naturalistic formulas appear less frequently and with less of a claim to authority. The typical "naturalistic" plot—a sequence of events ending in death and destruction—finds a counterpoint in motifs of regeneration, re-emphasized by the dramatic structure. *The Pit,* in particular, suggests that Norris was perhaps preparing to leave his entire "Naturalistic" armature behind, even as he turned his attention to the city of his birth and to a psychological drama of urban, educated, middle-class characters, characters more like himself, his family, and friends, than the protagonists of his earlier works.

The Pit would seem to be a watershed for Norris in a number of ways. More fully and directly than any of Norris's previous fiction, *The Pit* dramatizes the consequences for the self of the failure to recognize the inevitability of change, the impossibility of perfection, the ever-present reality of pain and loss, and the rewards of human contact. Even more than *The Octopus, The Pit* explores the possibility of moving through time and experience without either disintegrating in the process or stultifying oneself with defensive maneuvers. Finally, *The Pit* provides an image of the regenerative and integrative potential of memory and art. In fact, through Page's journal and her relationship with Landry Court, *The Pit* even projects, tentatively and comically, an image of the life-giving power of narrative.

Norris's fiction repeatedly explores the relationship between art and "life." From the beginning, his work is intermittently concerned with the genesis of verbal structures out of experience and with experience that is shaped and contained by verbal structures. To track the progress of these issues as explored within Norris's work is to perceive, in a sense, a unified vision—a vision as consistent and integrated as the philosophical assumptions that Donald Pizer extrapolates from Norris's novels, or as the pattern of aesthetic values analyzed by Don Graham. Yet the present analysis would not be complete without taking note of the irony with which Norris often complicates, and sometimes all but undercuts, his own single-minded commitment to a vision of experience shaped within and through narrative.

Norris's novels repeatedly dramatize life as storytelling and storytelling as both life and death. The vision is serious, often grim, especially when it suggests the destructive possibilities of the very element that elsewhere serves a stabilizing and potentially constructive function. No one knew better than Norris that fiction can stultify experience as well as integrate it. Yet pernicious or paralyzing elements coexist with comic or life-sustaining ones.

Once again, *Blix* provides a convenient paradigm, this time for the ironies and comic paradoxes in Norris's conception of narrative. Nothing could be more serious than Condy's own creative process—the only obsession in all Norris's work to purge itself fruitfully. Condy (and the novel as a whole) seem to glory in the very notion of "creation" through the word. Like Adam in the Garden of Eden (and like Norris with friends in his own life), Condy even "names" Blix, coining a new word for what seems to him an entirely original creature.

However, *Blix* is also full of comic or bizarre perspectives on fiction and creation. The diver's story is one extreme: narrative as order that is all but paralytic. Yet Blix and Condy's "creative" matchmaking venture dramatizes a different process, where fiction literally comes to determine the course of life itself.

Early in the novel, Condy peruses the morning paper and reads aloud to Blix from one of the advertisements:

> "Personal.—Young woman, thirty-one, good housekeeper, desires acquaintance respectable middle-aged gentleman. Object, matrimony. Address K.D.B., this office." (163)

Soon Blix and Condy conceive the notion of writing to K.D.B. in the name of "Captain Jack" whose own ad in the "personals" column announces his search for a "'respectable young woman, good housekeeper, and manager. Object, matrimony'" (164). "'Can't we fix it up some way . . . to bring these two together?'" Blix suggests (165).

> Condy smote the table and jumped to his feet.
>
> "Write to 'em!" he shouted. "Write to K.D.B. and sign it Captain Jack, and write to Captain Jack—"
>
> "And sign it K.D.B.," she interrupted, catching his idea.
>
> "And have him tell her, and her tell him," he added. "to meet at some place and then we can . . . hide, and watch."
>
> . . . .
>
> "Won't it be the greatest fun?"
>
> "Fun! Why, it will be a regular drama. Only we are running the show, and everything is real. Let's get at it!"
>
> Blix ran into her room and returned with writing material. . . .
>
> "Now," said Condy, "we must have these sound perfectly natural, because if either of these people smell the smallest kind of a rat, you won't catch 'em. . . . This is an art, a kind of fiction, don't you see?" (165–66)

Blix and Condy's little matchmaking "fiction" (which is a much greater success than Condy's story) could be called "A Victory Over Life." Yet the progress of this "real-life drama" is absolutely full of fictions. Condy and Blix fabricate a past for the red-haired man in the restaurant-meeting-place, imposing their scenario upon him. And Captain Jack himself relies heavily on storytelling in his wooing of K.D.B. After leaving the restaurant, K.D.B. and Captain Jack pass Condy and Blix in animated conversation. "'He was telling her of his adventures!' cried Blix. 'Splendid! Othello and Desdemona—They're getting on'" (199). When Condy is suddenly overtaken by misgivings about the possible consequences of the match, he expresses his fear to Blix: "'Suppose he kills her some time,'" he worries (198). But Blix's reference to Othello is not mainly a reference to Othello's murdering his wife. Rather, it recalls his own wooing of Desdemona with—what else—his narrated adventures. "I think this tale would win my daughter too," says the Duke of Venice after Othello describes the storytelling that won Desdemona's heart (*Othello,* I.3.171).

The relationship between "reality" and "fiction" is further complicated as the novel unfolds. After Condy and Blix become friends with the newlyweds, Blix raises the question of Captain Jack's veracity. She wonders out loud if he wasn't simply "'making all those things up as he went along. . . . He might have been lying, Condy'" Blix reflects (226). But this possibility doesn't worry Condy. "'What difference would that make?'" he asks. If Captain Jack plays fast and loose with actual facts, he has certainly married the right woman: K.D.B., methodically and assiduously memorizing the information in the encyclopedia, may prove to be a tempering influence.

Not since Norris's first published work, *Yvernelle,* his medieval verse romance in three cantos, have words had so much impact on events in "reality." *Yvernelle* begins with a curse; its entire plot hinges on the hero's effort to avert the life-destroying impact of the words directed against him. He ultimately succeeds in turning the destructive power of the curse back against the speaker herself. Thus, from his earliest writing, Norris gives serious treatment to the somewhat magical, often fearsome, power of words and the tales they tell.

The interplay of "fiction" and "reality" in *Blix* is more intricate and more playful than in Norris's other works. Within *Blix* the ironies cut so many ways that a stable perspective on either art or life is difficult to achieve, despite the unmistakable note of joyful gravity at the end of the book. The gamesomeness of *Blix* is less apparent elsewhere in Norris's work, where his mimetic assumptions and his affinities with the romantic tradition combine to project a vision of the evolving self engaged in a struggle for coherence and self-integration. Norris's depiction of that struggle would, in fact, seem to be grounded in a growing conviction that words can serve as a potentially reliable medium of expression, as a mode of communication with others, and as an aid in the creation of viable selves, as well as stories.

As Norris's fiction develops, the struggle for coherence is waged by particular characters with increasing success. The coherence of Norris's fiction—the narrative coherence—dramatically increases as well. By the time of *The Pit* (1903), Norris directly engages the problematics of the self, and he does so with a text that is virtually free of the narrative disjunctions of story and voice that burden his earlier works. Norris's first novels, on the other hand, especially *Vandover and the Brute,* exhibit considerable contradictions of this sort. As Vandover's own bid for coherence ends in failure, so the narrative coherence of the text that generates him is repeatedly threatened by warring elements within. To undertake analysis of *Vandover and the Brute,* then, is to encounter a pervasive problem of coherence, one that appears at several levels.

3. Vandover and the Brute: *The Failure of Memory and Art*

> Ah, he was no worse than the average; one could get accustomed to almost anything; it was only in the books that people had their lives ruined. . . .
>
> —Norris, *Vandover and the Brute*

> Nothing more could be done. The suffering had to go on, and he began to wonder how human beings could endure such stress and yet live.
>
> —Norris, *Vandover and the Brute*

Approximately six weeks after his father's death, installed in comfortable new surroundings, Vandover thinks about the "three great catastrophes" that had recently befallen him, "like the springing of three successive mines beneath his feet: Ida's suicide, the wreck [of the Mazatlan], and his father's death, all within a month" (437). At this juncture, just halfway through the novel, Vandover marvels at the suddenness of these events, since "[f]or nearly twenty-six years nothing extraordinary had happened to break in upon the uneventful and ordinary course of his existence" (437). It is striking, in this context, that he does not recall his mother's death, eighteen years earlier, although the text suggests that this event interrupted his "uneventful and ordinary existence" with some force.

The death of Vandover's mother is a crucial incident in *Vandover and the Brute*. It is Vandover's only detailed childhood memory. An extended description of his mother's final moments is first presented in the opening pages of the novel. After a train journey that had been "too much for her" (282), Vandover's mother lies back on pillows in a "steamer chair" and suddenly sighs deeply. While the eight-year-old Vandover watches, his mother's face becomes blank, and her head rolls forward, saliva dripping from her lower lip. We are told that the "scene of her death was the only thing that Vandover could remember of his mother" (283).

Vandover repeatedly recalls his impression of this moment, which is the earliest rendered incident in his chronological "history,"[1] and which is given considerable prominence in the text. Yet the narrative voice explicitly minimizes the significance of the event. Indeed, throughout the novel, the narrative voice suggests that Vandover has adapted thoroughly—even too easily—not only to this particular loss but to the experience of loss in general. Vandover, both in conversation with other characters and in internal monologues, expresses a similar sense of his excessive adaptability.

Such a reading of Vandover's character, however, is repeatedly undercut by countercurrents in the text. At its most imaginatively coherent, *Vandover and the Brute* is the story of a self crippled by a loss it can neither integrate nor transcend. That self is thus condemned to relive its deprivation repeatedly in one form or another. The pronouncements of the narrative voice in *Vandover* tend to blur this fact or to deflect attention from it. Vandover's own reflections are no more illuminating with regard to his actions or motives. Yet we need not take at face value either Vandover's commentary or that of the narrative voice. The issues implicit in the action cohere sharply once we focus instead on the events of the plot and the pattern of recurring motifs.

The problem of sudden loss is the imaginative center of the novel and it is an issue with far-reaching implications. All the weaknesses recurrently attributed to Vandover—his pliable character, his self-indulgence, his need for amusement—become more comprehensible when seen in the light of this issue. The plot of *Vandover* is punctuated by losses, usually losses through death. Vandover loses his mother, Ida Wade, many of his fellow passengers on the Mazatlan, his father, and Turner Ravis, as well as his entire social world, his art, and finally all his money and possessions. However, neither Vandover nor the narrative voice stresses the impact of these losses upon him. Both emphasize, instead, Vandover's prodigious adaptability to the experience of loss, trouble, and change.

Such contradictory emphases, pervasive within *Vandover and the Brute,* are typical of a problem I have already noted, a problem present throughout Norris's work. Particularly in Norris's early fiction, the narrative voice tends to offer interpretive comments as the events of the plot unfold. I have suggested that these discursive formulations, often cast in the familiar terms of philosophical naturalism, generally fail to provide an adequate frame for the dramatic events. Here, as elsewhere, such a frame can be found in the issue of coherent, or incoherent, selfhood.

In *Vandover,* the perspective created upon the death of Vandover's mother affords an illuminating point of departure for closer consideration of disjunctures within the text. Throughout the novel, Vandover's "pliable character" is said to be one of his greatest weaknesses.[2] Yet if one considers Vandover's "adaptability" in the light of his actions and his thoughts throughout the text, one finds that far from being too "pliable," Vandover's character and his own view of events assume their firm, even definitive shape in the death scene of Chapter I. The initial rendering of Vandover's response to sudden loss—his rolling eyes, frozen physical posture and suppressed emotional reaction—becomes a model for the text's representation of his later reactions to analogous experiences. Moreover, Vandover's behavior, thoughts, and feelings throughout the novel may be seen to approximate, with near textbook simplicity, those of a child who has been incomprehensibly abandoned and who takes that abandonment (and all future abandonments) as a deserved punishment for his own badness.

Thus, the death of Vandover's mother is decisive both for Vandover's emotional development and for the structure and imaginative coherence of the text that he inhabits. Vandover consistently takes key events in his life as bolts out of the blue. His reaction to his father's death is typical in this respect. "'You know,'" his lawyer reminds him, when Vandover's father dies, "'We've all been expecting—been fearing—that for some time'" (422). Still, for Vandover, his father's death, like Ida's, has the impact of a sudden explosion (437).

Vandover reacts with surprise and incredulity to all events that overtake him, with the incredulity and bewilderment of a child who at one level assumes he has no power to shape his own experience, yet who at another level feels he is responsible for everything that happens to him. Although Vandover believes he has no control over anything, he also feels that everything that happens to him is his own fault. If this would seem to be a contradiction, it is only one of the many contradictions informing Vandover's view of life and the novel's presentation of his experience.

The organizing issues in Vandover's story are consistently obscured by the interpretive comments of the narrative voice, even as they are shown to be fatally obscured in Vandover's own consciousness. If the novel's discourse about adaptability is misleading, so are most of its other generalizing statements, whether about particular events in the plot, Man's duality, or the "irresistible forces of Nature."

The various formulations about Vandover's memory reveal paradigmatic contradictions. The first paragraph of the novel is devoted to Vandover's own sense of the randomness of memory. Vandover is said to be chronically incapable of imposing any coherence on "the story of his life" (281). Insofar as he is capable of remembering his past at all, his memory is said merely to have "preserved [a few disconnected incidents] with the greatest capriciousness, absolutely independent of their importance" (281).[3] The notion of Vandover's "capriciousness" supports the assertion that Vandover's repeated recollection of his mother's death is accounted for by a mere "wilful fillip" of Vandover's "arbitrary" memory.

Many elements in the text, however, contradict the statement that Vandover's memory is arbitrary. Apart from the death of his mother, the only childhood incident that Vandover recalls "with any degree of clearness" occurred five years afterward and "was one of the greatest triviality[,] in which he saw himself, a rank thirteen-year-old boy, sitting on a bit of carpet in the back yard of the San Francisco house playing with his guinea-pigs" (283). This memory, though minimal, is far from random. For if Vandover's first childhood memory recalls the loss of his mother, his second one presents a muted image of mothering. Van, playing with his guinea pigs, is implicitly tending them and taking pleasure in them—as he never remembers either his mother or his father having done for him.

It is impossible to say why the narrator fails to emphasize the connection between Vandover's only two childhood memories, or to establish whether Norris himself was fully aware of the interrelations thus implied. Nonetheless, the novel subtly proceeds to reemphasize and extend them.

Like the idea of Vandover's "fatal adaptability," or the idea of his arbitrary memory, the reiterated notion of Van's self-indulgence can be fully understood only in relation to the story implied by the far from "trivial" memories Vandover has preserved. Throughout the book, one of Van's few purposive activities is his search for the comfortable environments that he provides for himself and within which he dozes "between the warm sheets; . . . [and] over[feeds] himself" (440) like a too-protected baby. When Geary comes to see Vandover with the news of Ida's death, he finds Van characteristically cocooned in his bathtub, dozing, "with his novel on a rack in front of him and a box of chocolates [and cigarettes] conveniently near" (368). It is not the only time that Vandover will be expelled from a warm tub by trouble, or will retreat from trouble into one.[4] His persistent concern for his window seat, his tiled stove, his sweets, food, drink, and tobacco creates a vivid image of compensatory self-mothering.

Although his mother's death is one of Vandover's few childhood memories, he fails to place it within any wider context. It remains one of several isolated images that linger beneath the threshold of his consciousness, surfacing now and again—at random, as he sees it. Moreover, insofar as we gain access to Vandover's memory of his mother's death, he formulates no immediate response; indeed, he utters no sound. Virtually all later losses, however, beginning with Ida Wade's death (371–72), elicit two reactions not noted in relation to the death of Vandover's mother: guilt, and the wish to scream with fear.

As the novel unfolds, Van is subject both to steadily increasing guilt and to bouts of mounting terror. It seems to be an objectless terror that overtakes Vandover, and the less he understands it, the more frightening it becomes. "He was afraid of this fear that was afraid of nothing" (490). However, this "terror . . . without any assignable reason" (490), turns out to be fear of the unspecifiable itself, the "unreasoning terror of something unknown" (521, 551).

Within *Vandover and the Brute* (as throughout Norris's fiction), characters are subject to acute fear of the unknown. In an early scene a group of Vandover's friends, gathered at the house of Turner Ravis, discusses an earthquake that had occurred the night before. When Van comes in they are "all talking at the same time" (310), each with a different opinion about the precise time of the earthquake. The intensity of the discussion suggests that fixing the time of the event is an act of some importance for the characters, perhaps because one can do nothing about earthquakes themselves.

Only a few pages later, the same group of friends is shaken by another event over which it has no control. Turner begins to tell the story of a glass that had incomprehensibly broken in her mother's hand that morning, when suddenly

> the very glass she held in her hand at the moment cracked and broke in precisely the manner she was describing.
>
> Turner drew in a long breath, open-mouthed, her hand in the air still holding the body of the glass that had remained in her fingers. They all began to exclaim over the wonder. (312)

Only Geary "refuse[s] to be carried away by their excitement" (313), coming forward quickly with a "scientific" explanation, just as he had provided an apparently irrefutable argument in assigning a time to the earthquake. However, the group of young people remains unsettled in the presence of "strangeness" (313) it can neither explain nor control. "It was some little time before they could get over their impression of queerness" (314).

Vandover's terror of the unexpected or unknown goes far beyond that of any other character. For Van, a known situation, however grim, is always preferable to change. Thus, after the wreck of the Mazatlan, when Van takes his seat in a lifeboat, he looks down at the sea and then makes

> an involuntary movement to regain the ship's deck. . . . It seemed simple madness to attempt to launch the boat; *even the sinking wreck would be safer than this change*. Vandover was terrified. (399, my emphasis)

Unlike Geary, who "always look[s] out for rain" (453), Vandover is repeatedly caught off guard, consumed by the fear of hidden mines beneath his feet. At the same time, Van's fear of the unknown is related to his unspecific guilt.

"'What have I done? What have I done *now*?'" (370, my emphasis), says Vandover immediately after learning of Ida Wade's suicide. Throughout the novel, Vandover is susceptible to "wild, hysterical terror" (477), preoccupied with imminent, unspecific threats, perpetually afraid of encountering an unexpected blow, like the one that revolutionized his world at the time of his mother's death. Like the bereaved eight-year-old he once was, the older Van takes such blows to be at once incomprehensible and entirely deserved. The component of guilt in Vandover's fear repeatedly surfaces.[5]

The loss of Ida, his father, and Turner all elicit the same reaction in Vandover; grief sooner or later gives way to a period of self-castigation (370, 469). Vandover summarizes it unambiguously for himself after Turner's rejection:

> . . . he had killed his father, estranged the girl he might have loved, outraged the world, and at a single breath blighted the fine innate purity of his early years. (471)

Soon he finds himself for the first time unable to paint, and he clearly takes the failure of his artistic power as another loss for which he is wholly responsible. "It was gone—his art was gone. . . . That, too, like all the other good things of his life, he had destroyed" (481). Gripped by terror, he rolls his eyes as he had done in the fatal train station of the novel's opening pages (compare 282).

Shortly afterward, Vandover is plunged into a "torment . . . [a] crisis [which does] not pass off" (p. 491), and in which

> [a]t first the room looked unfamiliar to him, then his own daily life no longer seemed recognizable, and, finally, all of a sudden, it was the whole world, all the existing order of things, that appeared to draw off like a refluent tide, leaving him alone, abandoned, cast upon some fearful, mysterious shore. (491–92)

Once Vandover feels abandoned by his art, he compares "this last calamity" to the experience of a parent, bereaved by the loss of a child: "[S]ome dear, sweet child, that might have been his companion throughout all his life" (483).[6] Soon, however, we find the experience converted to its prototype. Vandover does not, in fact, feel like a bereaved adult; rather, he feels like a motherless child, abandoned by "the whole world . . . upon some fearful, mysterious shore" (491–92)—like a figure in one of his own paintings.

Having once articulated his sense of abandonment, Vandover quickly and clearly interprets it:

> It was the *punishment that he had brought upon himself,* some fearful nervous disease, the result of his long indulgence of vice, his vile submission to the brute that was to destroy his reason. (493, my emphasis)

Vandover's conclusion here is the logical outcome of his consistent assumption that he deserves every threat, blow, and loss to which he is subjected. Throughout the text, the narrator supports Vandover's sense of culpability. Indeed, here as elsewhere, Vandover's view and that of the narrative voice are all but indistinguishable.

As Vandover's nervous disease progresses, he arrives at a state of absolute indifference. Perhaps, once he has encountered what he takes to be his long-awaited punishment, Vandover is relieved. His indifference certainly enables him to endure loss with more apparent equanimity than ever before. At the end of Chapter XV, Vandover succumbs to the manipulations of his old friend Geary; he sells his Mission Block property to Geary at a fraction of its value in order to avoid a courtroom battle with Ida Wade's father. Shortly thereafter, when Vandover's furniture is impounded because of unpaid bills, he sells his last property holding—his father's former house. We learn that Vandover "parted from his old home with as much indifference as he had parted from his block in the Mission" (525).

Vandover's gambling begins just at this point. It is almost as if, now that Vandover has become so very good at enduring loss, he can "play" at winning and losing. In doing so, he at once tempts fate to defeat him and, in a sense, removes the issue from the realm of his own life-choices, from the question of his own worthiness, or from the issue of reward and punishment. Vandover's gambling is "only" a game, at least at first. His passion for gambling grows quickly, however, and soon he plays for ever greater stakes. "Here at last, was the new pleasure for which he had longed, the fresh violent excitement that alone could . . . amuse him" (532). Before long gambling becomes "Vandover's only pleasure" (533).

Vandover's gambling follows logically upon his previous experience of life; here the imaginative coherence of the novel is impressive. As in the case of Vandover's alleged "adaptability" and his "capricious" memory, however, the narrator's notion of Vandover's "need for amusement," for "the excitement of the moment" (534), merely obscures the logic of Van's degeneration.[7] In one sense Vandover's motive for gambling is easy to see; here at last is a chance for him to win. It is, moreover, a chance based on chance, which thus gives Vandover the feeling that the odds might just possibly be in his favor—as they never seem to be in "real" life, where he only (as he sees it) deserves to lose.

We could, however, put the matter otherwise. Having reached the point of total indifference to loss, life is intolerable to Vandover. Loss was the focal point of his experience. One might say that without the threat of loss, Vandover has nothing to live for. It is in this sense a stroke of genius that Vandover finds a framework within which to encounter losses regularly. For it is in fact the chance to lose, rather than the chance to win, that would seem to make gambling so irresistible to Vandover. Vandover's gambling becomes a true passion, a mania, not when he is winning, but precisely when he "continued to lose, for his ill luck was extraordinary" (534).[8]

To some degree, then, Vandover's reactions to threat and loss throughout the novel are based on the model of the silent, passive, abandoned child of his memory in Chapter I. However, by the time Van loses all his remaining money, his need to express panic culminates in a "wild, hysterical desire to rush through the streets screaming and waving his arms" (541). This graphic image suggests a considerable store of unexpressed feelings.[9]

In a sense, Norris's entire depiction of Vandover dramatizes an attempt (or a failure) to come to terms with terror, an aborted effort to master (or simply to express) the feelings elicited by the unknown or unexpected, the sudden event that in Vandover's rendered experience has repeatedly led to loss. Vandover's full reaction, however, never finds effective expression. He "shut[s] his teeth against [the desire to scream]" (541; compare 372), just as he fails to execute his conception for a great painting.

We have seen that much of Vandover's behavior throughout the novel seems related to childhood experiences he does not remember in detail and rarely reexamines or reflects upon. Vandover's represented experience receives its essential shape, not through his conscious reflections but through his minimal memories, and through his unreflecting reenactment, or occasional revision, of certain aspects of his past. Vandover's fate thus appears to be determined by his own undigested experience. This point can help illuminate Vandover's relation to art.

Throughout *Vandover and the Brute* art is seen obliquely and tentatively as a potential tool for the integration of experience. Although Vandover does not try to write or tell his own story, he does struggle with his painting, and his painting becomes an important index of his success or his failure to impose imaginative form upon his experience. It is this struggle to which the text alerts us at the very start by emphasizing Vandover's failure to impose coherence on the "story of his life."

Vandover's artistic talent is said to be for painting and drawing. He particularly excels in two specific areas. He draws "nude women better than anyone in the school, perhaps better than anyone in the city . . . his feeling for the flesh, and for the movement and character of a pose, was admirable" (336). Apart from this, his best work consists of

> broad reaches of landscape, deserts, shores, and moors in which he placed solitary figures of men or animals in a way that was very effective—as, for instance, a great strip of shore and in the foreground the body of a drowned sailor; a lion drinking in the midst of an immense Sahara; or . . . a dying war horse wandering on an empty plain. . . . (334)

Surely Vandover's choice of subjects is meaningful. The specification of what Vandover paints reveals that his "effective" paintings, with their "solitary figures," contain no images of living human beings. Instead, his barren landscapes contain nothing but animals or corpses. Only in his "idea for a great picture . . . his first masterpiece" (334), does he conceive of a live figure within a desolate expanse. But this picture is never completed. Though Vandover is very good at capturing the likeness of a given model, he cannot generate a live human figure by the force of his own imagination.

The difficulties encountered by Vandover in the process of executing his "masterpiece" are perhaps related to problems that plagued Norris in the writing of this novel. As Vandover cannot define for himself the meaning of the scene he would depict, Norris may have been unable to resolve the contradiction between his impulse to account ideologically for Vandover's degeneration and his imaginative projection of Vandover's experience in terms that subvert such accounting. Norris's rendering of Vandover's decline implies an imaginative grasp of human experience that strongly suggests Freud's view, although it is never directly formulated in Freudian terms. A keen intuition rather than a conceptual grasp of psychological process consistently informs Norris's best work. Indeed, we have seen that his intuition often collided with his conceptualizations, naturalist and otherwise.

As Vandover works on his "masterpiece," he experiences a conflict of his own. In particular, he cannot resolve the soldier's attitude to death:

> The effects [Vandover] wished to produce were isolation and intense heat; as to the soldier, he was as yet undecided whether to represent him facing death resignedly, calmly, or grasping the barrel of his useless rifle, determined to fight to the last. (334)

The possibilities Vandover considers for the soldier differ sharply from his own attitudes. Unlike the first possibility (the soldier's steadfast calm), Vandover is subject to rising hysteria in the face of threat as the novel unfolds. Unlike the second possibility (the soldier's readiness to fight to the last) Vandover faces desolation and even the threat of extinction with ever-increasing passivity. Loss and isolation are familiar to Vandover, but in his art (as in his life) he is incapable of forming a stable response to the difficult challenges that these experiences present.

Vandover is said to have "no idea of composition" in his work. He is very good at capturing the flesh tones or the pose of nude models in the "life class," just as he quickly becomes "to all outward appearances a typical Harvardian" in Cambridge (294), or effectively imitates certain aspects of his lawyer's apartment when he decorates his own sitting room.[10] But Vandover cannot compose, cannot sufficiently shape, his artistic material, just as he cannot actively shape his experiences, either in action or in memory.

The narrator, as Don Graham points out, subtly mocks Vandover's derivative conception of *The Last Enemy,* its source in the sentimental *Home Book of Art.*[11] But while the narrator's explicit evaluation is cogent in this case, it nonetheless obscures other meaningful aspects of Vandover's experiences. Vandover's repeated and always fruitless return to his conception of *The Last Enemy* dramatizes an unresolved tension. His picture remains unexecuted not only because Van's idea is too derivative but because it is too closely connected with feelings that remain inarticulate.

Norris's own shaping imagination, his capacity for composition, is far richer than that with which he endows his protagonist. A multitude of telling details in the novel (beginning with the choice of memories attributed to Vandover) makes an impressive design, a coherent, imaginative pattern. However, the implicit meaning of this pattern remains separate from, and often in contradiction with, the interpretations recurrently offered to the reader in the form of Vandover's reflections and other discursive passages.

It is impossible to say whether Vandover's unresolved relationship to his painting reflects Norris's uncertainty about the shape of his artistic material. But the conflict and failure that mark Vandover's artistic talent are certainly a measure of the relative stability and coherence of Vandover's "self." Vandover's most concerted effort to paint *The Last Enemy,* for example, is quite specifically rendered as an effort to resist self-destruction. However, as Vandover tries in this mood to paint his "masterpiece," he becomes "for the moment . . . a little child again" (467)—just as he does at the opera, earlier in the same chapter.[12]

> The lines on his canvas were those of a child just learning to draw; one saw for what they were intended, but they were crude, they had no life, *no meaning.* (476–77, my emphasis)

The implication here is that art can potentially provide "salvation," not through any magical sleight of hand, but insofar as it becomes a medium for giving meaning and shape to experience. For Vandover, of course, it fails to do so.

Vandover himself, sometimes distinct from the narrative voice, sometimes merging with it, often suggests that his art is the "one thing that could save him" (472; compare 462, 481).[13] In this case, however, unlike the case of Vandover's "capricious" memory or "pliable character," the recurrent formulation is supported by the structure of the dramatic action, as well as by many descriptive details throughout the text.

Vandover's final stint as an "artist" is to draw miniature pictures on iron safes.[14] This art surely cannot "save" him. Yet while producing these tiny landscapes, bereft of all human figures alive or dead, Vandover is "safe" indeed, still subject to the physical symptoms of his "nervous disease," but no longer subject to the feelings of terror that overtake him as he works on his large canvas. If Vandover's "safe" landscapes hold no promise, they also hold no threat.

As a boy, Vandover often prays "that he might become a great artist" (290). As a young man, after Turner's rejection, he harbors an elaborate fantasy of returning from abroad one day, acclaimed and renowned for his paintings (459–60). Instead, Vandover becomes a pathetic, inarticulate creature who says, "'Give me a dollar and I'll bark for you'" (573).

By the end of the novel Vandover in many ways has nothing left to lose, and yet once again the position he has achieved reveals the imaginative coherence of many elements within the text. If we are first introduced to Vandover through his "memory picture" of losing a good mother, we leave him in the hands of a mean stepfather who has robbed him of what is his and puts him to work, like Cinderella.

In the last chapter of the novel, Vandover has been cleaning one of Geary's rental cottages. As Vandover removes the filth left by the previous inhabitants, a family of prospective tenants begins to examine the house. The novel ends with a rather blatant juxtaposition between the wretched, pathetic Vandover and the future tenants' well-fed little boy. The boy stares in wonder as Vandover sits on the floor tying up his bundle of brush, rags, and broom.

The final tableau of *Vandover and the Brute* strikingly recalls its opening scene. In both, a wide-eyed little boy, about to change homes, watches something new and frightening within his experience.[15] The juxtaposition suggested by the novel's final image is not only between the ragged Vandover and the well-dressed little boy chewing bread and butter; it is a juxtaposition with additional implications. The novel begins with the young Vandover, who only dimly remembers the scene of his mother's death beside the noisy, smoking railroad train that was about to take his disintegrating family to an unknown place. The novel ends with a disheveled Vandover in the presence of a complacent little boy who is examining his prospective new home from a secure vantage point, within the bosom of a stable, even extended, family: his aunt is also present. The boy's parents openly relish the prospect of their latest move, and the conversation of mother, father, and aunt fluctuates between the pleasure they express in the details of the cottage and satisfaction in their respective children's talents and prospects in life. The boy's parents cherish his every word. "*There* was a smart little boy for you," they exclaim, after the child calls Vandover "you old lazee-bones." "You ought to see, he watched everything, and sometimes he'd plump out with things that were astonishing for a boy of his years" (589). As the boy's parents examine the cottage, ordering Vandover about, they recall various highlights of their child's development, such as "the first day he put on knickerbockers" (589).

The communication among the adults, including the way the mother and the aunt vie with one another over their children's virtues, provides a sharp contrast to the young Vandover of the novel's opening pages. The first words of the novel had pointed to Vandover's "wonder . . . that he was able to recall so little of his past life" (281). Certainly Vandover has had no mother, nor has he had the kind of father who would foster the retention or elaboration of memories. While the young Vandover remembers little of his past, and is convinced that such memories as he has retained have been "preserved with the greatest capriciousness," the family of the novel's closing scene panders to memory, fostering its own self-interest by preserving the story of its past.

We have seen how the text belies the notion that Vandover's memory has merely preserved "disconnected incidents . . . absolutely independent of their importance." Yet Vandover himself never becomes aware of the "story" implied by his own experience and by the content of his memories. At the end of the novel, as at the beginning, Vandover is unable to construct the story of his life either directly or indirectly. When he speaks of his recent past to Geary in the final chapter, the story he tells is quite incomprehensible—just as his effort to transform the stuff of his experience into art has degenerated into lines with "no meaning."[16]

By the end of the novel, however, Vandover has in a sense, without knowing it, "rewritten" his own life history. The novel's final image of Vandover is a revised version of Van at the start. We leave Vandover, in the final scene of the novel, having once again become "a little child"—now, however, not (as in Chapter XIV) only "for the moment." In the novel's closing pages, Vandover has become a very "good" boy, no longer the bad child of his conscience who "deserves" what he gets. When Vandover washes and cleans the windows of Geary's cottage in the last scene, he is "very careful not to disturb [the realty] . . . signs" (580). He works hard, talks respectfully to Geary, and doesn't complain (580, 582). The prospective tenant even rewards him for his diligence with a twenty-five-cent tip. Moreover, Vandover has put himself entirely in Geary's hands. In doing so, he has come full circle, and given up the struggle for either expression or mastery.

Vandover's story, then, rather than projecting an image of "fatal adaptability," may be seen as the dramatization of a failure to adapt to the stresses and changes of life. In this sense the hero of *Vandover and the Brute* would still appear to be perfectly cast in the mold of literary "naturalism." It thus becomes the more striking that Vandover's lack of adaptability fails to be amplified and clarified by the overtly "naturalistic" constructs within the text.

Various critics of Norris's work have viewed with some skepticism the notion that Vandover's decline can be explained by the "brute" within him, or by the split between his lower nature and his "better self." Again, while Vandover's "lycanthropy" might seem related to popular, contemporary theories of reversion or atavism, the imaginative coherence of *Vandover* stems more directly from Norris's vision of a self doomed to relive those aspects of its personal history with which it has not come to terms. In this sense, the novel seems to point more directly to Freud than to Darwin.

The Darwinian categories that intermittently appear throughout *Vandover* repeatedly shift in meaning according to their context; they cannot be uniformly interpreted. Just as moral categories become suspect when used by the priggish and self-interested Turner (whose morality, as Graham points out, does not prevent her from befriending Geary toward the end of the novel),[17] so naturalistic ideas shift in meaning according to the circumstances in which they appear.

The most notorious "Darwinian" passage in *Vandover,* for example, occurs in three separate places, with subtle differences; its implications are unresolvably ambiguous. In the first of these passages, the narrative voice, virtually indistinguishable from Vandover himself, speaks of "Life" as a

> great mysterious force that [spins] the wheels of Nature . . . like some enormous engine, resistless, relentless; . . . driving before it the infinite herd of humanity, . . . crushing out inexorably all those who lagged behind. (482)[18]

In the following chapter, it is Vandover himself who sees "Nature" as "inexorably exacting," inflicting "punishment" upon him. Vandover now sees himself as the victim of "the vast, fearful engine riding him down beneath its myriad spinning wheels, remorselessly, irresistibly" (493). Still later it is Geary, using precisely the same language, who reflects on the "infinite herd of humanity, driven on as by some enormous, relentless engine" (568). Geary quite explicitly uses these ideas to justify "his maxim," "[e]very man for himself" (568).

> All life was but a struggle to keep from under those myriad spinning wheels that dashed so close behind. . . . To lag behind was peril; to fall was to perish, to be ridden down, to be beaten to the dust, to be inexorably crushed and blotted out beneath that myriad of spinning iron wheels. Geary looked up quickly and saw Vandover standing in the doorway. (568–69)

The same language that allows Vandover to conceive of himself as a victim serves Geary's purposes in justifying his place in "the front rank." There is no doubt, of course, that Geary is successful while Vandover is crushed, ridden down, all but "blotted out," as his timely appearance in the wake of Geary's reflections confirms.

However, none of these ideas meaningfully elucidates Vandover's story, either by accounting for its contradictions or by integrating its disparate images and events. Like the idea of Vandover's "capricious memory" or "pliable character," the idea of the "resistless forces of Nature" becomes part of a litany that fails to provide a meaningful context for other elements in the novel. We cannot know whether Norris believed that the process of Vandover's decline is substantially clarified by the interpretive categories scattered through the text. There is no doubt, of course, that by the time Norris wrote *Vandover,* he had long been busy with theories of degeneration, reversion, atavism, and life-forces. Yet to take note of Norris's familiarity with such concepts is not to explain his relationship to them.

The prototype for Vandover is a story by Norris called "Lauth" (1893) in which a small group of scientists successfully resurrect a corpse, only to find him subsequently plunging down the evolutionary ladder in a process of graduated, ghastly decay. Lauth moves through Vandover's wolflike state to a still more primitive condition, like that of "the protozoa, the jellyfish, and those strange lowest forms of existence wherein the line between vegetable and animal cannot be drawn" (145).

Before undertaking the terrible task of tampering with death, one of the characters in the story explicitly indicates that the project seems "repulsive and wicked" to him. Anselm does not believe that the attempt to revive life can succeed, and while he confesses to "no little curiosity," he insists that "whatever happens, I shall regard it from a purely scientific, not from a religious standpoint. To me it is an experiment in physiology, not in psychology. I believe the soul, and only the soul, is the motor of existence" (134). At the end of the story, after the decomposition and death of "the thing," Anselm reaffirms his belief in the soul without which a man "is no longer a man" (147).

Without the scientific and religious framework, Anselm cannot countenance an undertaking that he sees as "repulsive and wicked." Perhaps the interpretive, pseudo-scientific formulations in *Vandover* serve an analogous function for Norris: making Vandover's grim decline more tolerable for his creator. The idea of the soul, central in "Lauth," plays no such role in *Vandover,* but the idea of "force" remains. Norris either could not or would not imagine Vandover's undoing without his conceptual scaffolding. Perhaps, like Anselm,

Norris could not renounce the need to explain, to account for, a process that would otherwise have seemed unbearable even to contemplate.

I have been suggesting that *Vandover* is strongest precisely where its pattern of recurrent motifs runs counter to the formula elsewhere offered in explanation. It is not the interpretive formulations but Vandover's inarticulate response to his mother's death that becomes the structural spine of the novel, the backdrop for a host of dramatic and descriptive details. The notion of adaptability itself gains meaning and derivation when seen not in relation to Darwinian categories, but in relation to the opening pages of the text. The end of the novel, like the train station scene at the beginning, projects an evocative image of the unadaptable Vandover: inarticulate, wide-eyed, well-behaved, and passive in the face of desolation.

Vandover's own increasing passivity and incoherence reflects his inability to organize experience either in memory and consciousness or through expressive art. This process reaches its climax at the end of the novel, when Vandover, having failed to integrate or to transcend particular aspects of his past, recreates them, with some revision. In this context it is worth recalling that although *Vandover and the Brute* was published posthumously in 1914, it was written during the same period in Norris's life as *McTeague*. If *Vandover* dramatizes progressive incoherence and unconscious reenactment as a response to change and loss, *McTeague* may be seen to depict a different outcome of analogous processes.

McTeague, Norris's first major fictional achievement, provides a panorama of responses to trouble and flux that are closely related to the notion, in *Vandover,* of disastrous experience obliquely and compulsively relived. At the same time, Vandover's ineffective, but potentially constructive, exploration of a different possibility—of salvation through art, through aesthetic form—is replaced in *McTeague* by a range of rigid habits and obsessions. Some of these, like Maria's reiterated story, or Trina's interminable carving of miniature Noah's Arks, may be seen as grotesque inversions of the aesthetic, ordering impulse. The various repetitive activities within *McTeague* merely serve to create the illusion of stability for the fearful and vulnerable self. However, after *McTeague,* and especially in *Blix, The Octopus,* and *The Pit,* Norris's fiction again considers the constructive possibilities of memory and art. And it does so with diminishing reliance on the overt interpretive formulations that come so close to undermining the imaginative and aesthetic force of *Vandover and the Brute.*

4. *Loss, Habit, Obsession: The Governing Dynamic of* McTeague

> "Oh, I can swim all right as long as papa holds my chin up. Soon as he takes his hand away, down I go."
>
> —Trina in Norris's *McTeague*

> [Miss Baker's] agitation betrayed itself in the repetition of the word.
>
> —Narrative voice in *McTeague*

McTeague (1899), the first of Norris's major novels to be published, was pivotal in winning him a place within the naturalist canon. From the novel's first appearance, readers generally assumed that the organizing principle behind the disparate stories of Trina and McTeague, Maria and Zerkow, Old Grannis and Miss Baker, must lie in the large "naturalistic" themes implied by the sequence of events, and elucidated by narrative pronouncements about chance, instinct, atavism, heredity, and circumstance.[1] Seeking to account for the impact of the novel, recent critics of *McTeague,* like myself, have become increasingly suspicious of its naturalistic concepts and of readings that take the narrator's interpretive comments too literally.[2] Even without the "naturalistic" armature, however, the disparate characters and multiple actions of the text remain difficult to integrate within an organizing structure.

Yet the imaginative coherence of *McTeague* is impressive, and its coherence is not derived from naturalistic issues. The imaginative focus of *McTeague,* like that of *Vandover,* centers on the problem of personal loss and its implications for the self. Readers of *McTeague* have long taken the problem of greed as a crux, whether moral, psychological, or social. What animates this novel, however, is not the desperate lust for gain but the haunting fear of loss, to which greed is but one represented response within the text. *McTeague* is full of characters who are preoccupied with loss. Whatever a character may have lost, or feels in danger of losing, he tends to experience the potential or actual deprivation as a threat to the integrity of his being, as some kind of violation that opens the way to chaos or to death. Trina's hoarding of gold is only one among many strategies employed by the characters of *McTeague* to protect themselves from the experience of loss, or from the fear of disintegration that follows such experience.

Within the world of the novel, everyone fears the implications of change and loss; the threatened self turns for protection to whatever stabilizing structures it can generate. In the effort to stabilize internal or external flux, McTeague drinks steam beer, smokes his pipe, and repeatedly plays the same six tunes on his concertina; Trina and Zerkow hoard gold; Old Grannis binds books; Maria Macapa incessantly repeats a phrase and a story; Papa Sieppe organizes and reorganizes his household, labeling, counting and fretting. *McTeague* is full of habits and obsessions, great and small, all serving to defend the self from whatever may threaten to subvert it in the present, or to buttress it against the reverberations of some threat experienced in the past. To consider *McTeague* in these terms is both to elucidate the logic of McTeague and Trina's decline and to perceive new connections between the novel's subplots and the story of the central protagonists.

Donald Pizer's analysis of Norris's concern with the turbulence "beneath the surface of our placid, everyday lives" has long been useful to students of American naturalism.[3] Trina's intrusion into the midday serenity of Polk Street with the news of Maria's brutal murder is only one of many scenes in *McTeague* where the commonplace surface of life is disrupted by a sudden revelation of its turbulent depths. But the notion of contrast between surface and depth can most clearly reveal the vital center of *McTeague* insofar as the juxtaposition implies an ongoing process in which the commonplace trappings and routines of daily life serve directly, though not always effectively, to stabilize and neutralize hidden turmoil, whether within the individual, or in his surroundings.

The novel's opening description of McTeague himself, cradled and supported by his immediate environment, implies a typical strategy for dealing with the threat of internal and external turbulence—a strategy Norris had previously employed in his depiction of Vandover's self-coddling. Throughout *McTeague,* the life of routine, full of forms and habits on which one can rely, becomes the protective bulwark of the vulnerable self as it struggles to ward off conflict and danger.

McTeague's habits are characteristic. Consider his favorite song: "No one to love, none to Caress, left all alone in this world's wilderness." McTeague tends to sing this song at what would seem to be peculiarly inappropriate moments: for example, while preparing for his wedding (118). But his singing is not inappropriate at all. What he sings is what he fears from the beginning, and he has every reason to do so. His fear of being "left all alone in the world's wilderness" will be literally fulfilled at the end of the novel. Moreover, his song suggests the paradigmatic tension of *McTeague*: chaos provisionally contained within a stabilizing medium. McTeague's inarticulate fear of loss is simultaneously articulated and effectively neutralized by its expression in a self-limiting, dependably repeatable form.

It is not just McTeague who moves from provisional stability to fear and violence beyond the routines of men and, indeed, beyond the rule of law; all the characters travel analogous routes, or barely avoid them. The fate of McTeague, left alone in the "[c]haotic desolation" (321) of Death Valley, has its analogue in the fate of Marcus, Trina, Maria, and Zerkow, all of whom intuitively apprehend and struggle against their own vulnerability from the beginning of the novel.

As the characters of *McTeague* struggle for balance, shelter, and self-definition, structures of habit sometimes do appear to afford a measure of stability. When the structure breaks down, however, two basic possibilities emerge. One possibility, projected through the story of Old Grannis and Miss Baker, is for the self, so to speak, to go it alone, to trust its spontaneous impulses, and to risk exposing itself to others. The second possibility, more common in *McTeague,* is for the self to seek stronger measures of control. A life of habit tends to give way to one of obsession, especially when danger arises despite the defensive structure that has seemed to contain it. In the face of imminent threat, obsession would seem to narrow the range of complexity, internal and external, with which the self must cope. The process by which obsession comes to supplant a structure of habit is exemplified both in the story of Maria and Zerkow and in that of McTeague and Trina.

Maria Macapa, the Latin American maid-of-all-work, provides one of the sharpest examples of the pattern.[4] To ask Maria her name is to elicit the words "'Maria—Miranda—Macapa. . . . Had a flying squirrel an' let him go'" (15). Maria's other salient quality—her perpetual readiness to talk about her family's lost dishes—is equally automatic and habitual.

Both of Maria's repetitive responses center on loss: the squirrel has flown, the gold dishes have disappeared. Though Maria's losses are never fully explained, the details do not matter, nor does it make much difference whether the lost dishes are real or imaginary. The structure of Maria's preoccupation is clear, and her habits, in both form and function, are typical within *McTeague.*

Like McTeague's song, which evokes fear of desolation only to neutralize it, Maria's two habits at once refer to loss and serve to stabilize its effects. Any feelings that Maria's losses might have stirred are presumably neutralized by the stabilizing mechanism. Indeed, her nametag and her storytelling habits are harmless insofar as they are wholly self-contained. Only when passed on to Zerkow does Maria's story become an expanding obsession.

Everyone in *McTeague* is amused by Maria's habits. Various characters elicit her story for diversion. Only Zerkow sees Maria's habits in another light. Because her story engages Zerkow's own *idée fixe* (gold was "his dream, his passion . . . his consuming desire" [32]), Maria's story has for him a terrifying seriousness. If Maria's habit is soothing and stabilizing for Maria, it threatens utterly to subvert Zerkow's precarious balance. Only Zerkow tries to extend what had been a fixed monologue. "'Where did it all go to? Where did it go?'" he asks. "Maria shook her head. 'It's gone, anyhow'" (47). The question does not exist for Maria. The habit has in effect been adopted to deflect the unanswerable question.

The very dependability of Maria's narrative would seem to help limit Zerkow's own mania. The delicate balance is tipped when, after the death of her newborn child, Maria completely forgets her story. Maria's amnesia is illuminating both in its causes and in its effect. Zerkow has assumed that somehow Maria's story would one day lead him to the lost treasure (176). When Maria can no longer provide the story, Zerkow quite simply feels robbed. The withdrawal of the stabilizing framework transforms his relatively harmless delusion into a lethal fixation. In Zerkow, as elsewhere in *McTeague,* loss becomes a pivot in the movement from habit to obsession.

Maria's loss of memory, however, is also significant in another way.[5] Conceiving a child, giving birth to it, and seeing it die implicates Maria—despite her protective mechanisms—in life and death processes, processes of change (give and take, gain and loss) that her habit has partially protected her from. Ultimately Maria's habit fails to shield her from exposure to another person and from implication in the basic processes of life and death; ironically, in fact, it draws her into such exposure by speaking to the hidden depths of another being. Since Maria's habits have tended to insulate as well as to define her, her intimate contact both with another person and with uncontrollable flux releases her from her insulating mechanism. In Freudian terms, the loss of her "real" child may be seen to displace her need for the story of loss, whether real or imaginary. Because of the nature of Zerkow's own mania, however, Maria does not live to reap the potential rewards of her release. In fact, once she is "freed" of her preoccupation, she becomes more vulnerable than ever before: the loss of her habit leads directly to her death.

Maria's habits, stabilizing and defining her, make her a kind of Dickensian grotesque,[6] but also a known quantity, easily identifiable both by readers of the novel and by characters within it. Nonetheless, the characters of *McTeague* are baffled by Maria's habit, which they take to be "strange," a source of legends, a minor mystery (15–16). Their lack of understanding is typical within the novel. As others wonder at the strangeness of Maria's habit, Maria questions Old Grannis:

> "What you alus sewing up them books for, Mister Grannis?" asked Maria. . . . "There's just hundreds of 'em in here on yer shelves; they ain't no good to you."

> "Well, well," answered Old Grannis, timidly, rubbing his chin, "I—I'm sure I can't quite say; a little habit, you know; a diversion, a—a—it occupies one, you know." (26)

Although the story of Old Grannis and Miss Baker has consistently been seen as the most anomalous subplot of *McTeague*,[7] it fits clearly into the pattern of loss implicit in the novel. Like Maria's habits, or the organizational frenzies of Papa Sieppe,[8] Old Grannis's routine, especially his bookbinding, serves to insulate him from exposure to others and to protect him both from sudden changes in his environment and from troublesome impulses within himself.

The logic of Old Grannis's unique position within *McTeague* becomes clear in the light of Maria's marriage to Zerkow, her implication in life-processes, and her sudden, unexpected loss of habit. Old Grannis, alone in the novel, gives up his habit willingly. After selling his bookbinding apparatus, however, he is suddenly bewildered: there is a vacuum where a stable pattern used to be. He receives a large check and returns to his room, "sad and unoccupied"; he does not know what to do with his hands. "[F]or Old Grannis all was different that evening. There was nothing for him to do" (236).

Without habit to stabilize self and immediate environment, Old Grannis faces a void. But luckily for him, someone else intuitively grasps the implications of his habit and, therefore, what it means to him to give the habit up. Miss Baker responds generously to Old Grannis's loss and to his resulting desolation.

If habits may be said to delimit the self, they may also provide access to it.[9] And, indeed, Old Grannis and Miss Baker are said "to know each other's habits" (12) from the outset. Because Miss Baker "knows" Old Grannis's habit, she understands the implications of his renunciation. Old Grannis himself, of course, does not at first realize this: "It did not appear to him that he could be the same to Miss Baker now; their little habits were disarranged, their customs broken up" (237). Miss Baker, however, rises to the occasion, breaching her own structure of habit by entering Old Grannis's room with a cup of tea. "Never after could the little dressmaker understand how she had brought herself to do this thing" (237). No less than Trina's "sudden . . . unexpected . . . surrender of herself" (65) when she first kisses

McTeague, Miss Baker's own impulsive act astounds her. From her own point of view, "[i]t was an enormity" (238).

From Maria's question about Old Grannis's habit to his sale of the bookbinding apparatus, the old people's self-encapsulating habits are slowly but surely undermined. Old Grannis and Miss Baker are repeatedly agitated by challenges to their ritual of carefully controlled proximity. By the same token, of course, they are secretly gratified by the contact they fail to escape.

The Old Folks' structure of habit protects them both from the instabilities of the surrounding world and from their own wish for and fear of contact with one another. The unexpected can threaten inner balance from without, as Marcus does when he threatens to run down the stairs naked ("'Look out, now, here I come again. Not even a porous plaster on me this time'" [46]); but the unexpected can also arise from within. Though the Old Folks generally contain their unruly impulses, Miss Baker drops her groceries when she meets Old Grannis on the stairs; at the McTeague wedding, she addresses him directly without having intended to do so. Certain precautions, moreover, are not taken: "'Well,' Marcus would shout [with some justice] 'shut your door, then, if you don't want to see'" (46).

Indeed, the Old Folks are not as self-encapsulated as they seem. Their doors remain slightly ajar not only to Marcus's possible nakedness but also to each other, and they are virtually the only characters in *McTeague* who apprehend the vulnerability or pain of another being. Old Grannis alone understands the meaning of loss to Trina at the furniture auction; in fact, he buys McTeague and Trina's wedding photograph in order to give it to them as a present (207). Thus, it is not surprising that Old Grannis finds happiness when he renounces his system of self-fortification. "At last it had come—come when he had least expected it" (239).

The loss of one's timeworn occupation—the disruption of habit—opens a wedge to the unexpected. Everywhere else in *McTeague* this tends to mean chaos or obsession. For Old Grannis and Miss Baker, however, habit has been a kind of constraint whose removal releases the flow of spontaneous feeling. The habits that have protected the Old Folks from the unexpected have also denied them the benefits of the unexpected. Old Grannis's loss of habitual occupation, unlike McTeague's, results in a kind of redemption.[10]

It is illuminating to consider the major characters of *McTeague*—McTeague and Trina—in the light of the Old Folks, Maria and Zerkow. Perhaps the greatest critical problem in *McTeague,* after that of incorporating the subplots, is that of Trina's transformation from a trim, orderly housekeeper to a driven, ravaged, obsessive miser. The text's occasional references to Trina's "instinct of hoarding" or to her "penurious ancestors" do not begin to provide a convincing explanation for the change. Criticism has been increasingly concerned with the apparent unaccountability of this shift.[11] However, Trina herself fears and envisions it at a very early stage, and the terms in which she does so are revealing.

After her parents' departure on her wedding night, Trina experiences turmoil, fear, and a sense of isolation. She feels "left . . . alone," "horribly alone" (131) in the "strange, vast flat" (132) with McTeague and her "new life" (131). Such feelings may be not unusual in a "young bride," and in fact, Trina quickly establishes a new routine. Chapter X evokes the steady rhythm of her day, which (like that of the Old Folks or of McTeague at the outset) creates an atmosphere of safety and manageability. Nonetheless, intermittently "Trina would pause in her work . . . her eyes . . . growing wide and thoughtful as she gazed, unseeing, out into the rain-washed street" (135).

On her wedding night, Trina says she is afraid, but of what she at first "could not tell" (132). A moment later, however, she identifies her fear: "'I'm afraid of *you,*'" she suddenly tells McTeague (133). But Trina's fear is not elaborated until the following chapter.

One day, having spent the "better part of the afternoon" in the soothing and meticulously ordered context of Miss Baker's room having tea, Trina returns home to the sight of McTeague, sprawled in his operating chair, asleep and snoring. She reacts with terror and runs weeping to her bed, envisioning the possibility that "she would . . . come to be like him, would sink to the level of steam beer and cheap tobacco, *and all her pretty ways, her clean, trim little habits* would be forgotten. . . . A great despair seized upon her" (136–37, my emphasis).

This scene exposes the true roots of Trina's fear.[12] Even more than McTeague singing his song of desolation, Trina intuitively anticipates the internal changes she herself will undergo long before she (or the reader) has any reason to do so. Trina's thoughts imply that she imaginatively apprehends the fragility of her "pretty ways, her clean, trim little habits," which are, in effect, her only bulwark against chaos.

If *McTeague* projects an image of man as a creature of habit, whose habits define him both to himself and to others, it is not surprising that Trina's terror of loss of self should be conceptualized in terms of loss of habit. In the novel's presentation of her character, Trina is more clearly defined by her "clean, trim little habits" than by anything else. These are also the qualities by which Trina knows herself and on which her sense of value and well-being depends. All this is threatened by her exposure to McTeague, not because he is more "primitive" than she,[13] but because, having accepted close contact with another being, Trina feels violated—and not only on the sexual level.

The sexual level is extremely important to be sure. Trina feels her autonomy has been threatened by McTeague partly because he has elicited her uncontrolled sexual responses. After Trina's marriage, says the narrative voice, "[w]ith the absolute final surrender of herself, the irrevocable, ultimate submission, had come an affection the likes of which she had never dreamed in the old B Street days" (135). The "final surrender" is sexual, of course, but for Trina, sexual surrender means surrender and submission of many kinds, culminating in her feeling that she has lost control and, therefore, lost herself. It is the meaning of surrender for Trina herself that accounts for her fear and finally for the conversion of her "little habits" into her uncontrollable obsession.

Trina is said to love McTeague after their marriage "because she had given herself to him freely, unreservedly, and had merged her individuality into his" (135). This is where Trina's terror comes in. She reacts with growing panic to this "free" giving of herself—a giving so free as to violate the very bounds of her individuality. Having given of herself, she fears for herself, afraid of losing first her pretty ways, her little habits, and then her very being.

"Was there not something gone from Trina now?" (62) McTeague reflects, after Trina surrenders to his kiss at the B Street station. The narrative voice notes the "barely perceptible . . . revulsion of feeling" in McTeague at this point. "Perhaps he dimly saw that this . . . belonged to the changeless order of things—the man desiring the woman only for what she withholds; the woman worshipping the man for that which she yields up to him" (62). Unlike narrative pronouncements about heredity and chance, these lines are usually dismissed as cliché, a sign of Norris's Victorian prejudices. They cannot be so easily dismissed, however. They harmonize too well with the language that emphasizes gain and loss within this scene and throughout the depiction of Trina. If McTeague vaguely feels that there is something "gone from Trina" after her surrender, Trina herself feels it with a vengeance. It is precisely for this reason that she later guards her money as, during her courtship, she guarded her sexual favors—and with far greater "success."[14]

Here, rather than in the vagaries of chance or in Trina's "penurious" ancestors, the source of Trina's gold-hoarding obsession may be seen in its full relation to the pervasive motifs within *McTeague*. After her first kiss, Trina feels she has been robbed. She thus begins to save another treasure, soon to be stored (appropriately enough) in a locked trunk beneath her bridal dress.

To Trina sexuality means inner chaos and dependency on another person, while greed appears to promise control and self-sufficiency. In the face of her "sudden . . . unexpected . . . surrender of herself" (65), Trina turns to her money with a fierce need to exercise proprietary control, such as she cannot achieve over either her inner self or her wider surroundings. Trina is "overpowered" by her greed, as by her sexuality. "'I can't help it,'" she says repeatedly. But her submission to what she considers her "good fault" leaves her with a temporary feeling of gain and control rather than with a sense of loss.

Throughout *McTeague,* when habit fails to provide the threatened self with adequate protection, stronger measures are invoked. Trina's "trim habits" do not sufficiently protect her from either internal or external change, neither from "that sudden unexpected surrender of herself" when she kisses McTeague nor from the sudden changes in her external circumstances suggested first by her winning of the lottery, and later by the letter that drops through McTeague's door to destroy his dental practice.

Trina buys the "lucky" lottery ticket on the morning she first meets McTeague. Both events have the same implications. Great gain stimulates fear of great loss, implying the vulnerability of the self. Trina's winning of the lottery, like her contact with McTeague, makes Trina fear her own impulses: to spend, to give, to let go. "'Oh Mac!' exclaimed Trina . . . 'think of all this money coming to us just at this very moment. Isn't it wonderful? Don't it kind of scare you?'" (89). Trina's windfall, moreover, suggests the possibility of sudden changes of fortune in general. Her good luck inevitably raises the specter of equally unexpected, adverse change.

At the imaginative heart of *McTeague* lies the problem of change, of gain and loss, and its implications for the precarious self. This issue directs the thrust of the entire novel and helps account for its impact. Naturally it also pervades the depiction of McTeague himself.

McTeague's rude habits, like Trina's "trim" ones, define him and give him a sense of well-being and self-recognition. But while McTeague at first appears stable, he really is not, for his stability depends upon the absolutely unalterable reliability of his routine. If he moves beyond the bounds of his well-defined structure, he is quickly at a loss. He cannot work and talk at the same time (14). When he ventures out to buy theatre tickets, he comes to feel virtually nullified. For a person so dependent on routine, any change may bring chaos in its wake.

At the start of the novel, McTeague, like the other characters, is introduced through his characteristic habits; thus, it seems fitting that disrupted habits should serve to define Trina's entry into his life. With his exposure to Trina in Chapter II, McTeague's

> narrow point of view was at once enlarged and confused, and all at once he saw that there was something else in life besides concertinas and steam beer. Everything had to be made over again. His whole rude idea of life had to be changed. (20)

After meeting Trina, McTeague finds that his structure of habit cannot contain all the elements of his experience. Moreover, throughout *McTeague,* when habit is suddenly disrupted, unless (as for the Old Folks) it means salvation, obsession is likely to be near.

> Little by little, by gradual, almost imperceptible degrees, the thought of Trina Sieppe occupied his mind from day to day, from hour to hour. He found himself thinking of her constantly; at every instant he saw her round, pale face; her narrow, milk-blue eyes; her little . . . chin . . . her heavy . . . black hair. (20)

Thus, the pattern pervading the novel is manifest right at the start. Disruption of habitual order may open the way to chaos, and one direct route to chaos is through uncontrollable obsession.

McTeague's own movement toward obsession is less direct than that of Trina or Zerkow. A revised structure of habit repeatedly restores McTeague's equilibrium after it has been undermined by a growing preoccupation. Once Trina has "surrendered" to McTeague, he is no longer obsessed with her. Indeed, after his marriage, McTeague soon becomes as passively contented as he was at the start of the novel, entrenched within the new order established by Trina. McTeague's acceptance of new habits (138) temporarily calms Trina's fears, while stabilizing his own position (140). A series of disruptive losses, however, transforms McTeague (like Trina and Zerkow) into a man obsessed.

When McTeague loses his right to practice dentistry, the stable shape of his day is destroyed. McTeague tries for a time to maintain the formal structure of his working day, despite its lack of content. In fact, it is not the substance but the form of a stable framework that matters to McTeague. Once it is clear that his structure of habit simply cannot be maintained, McTeague (like Old Grannis after selling his bookbinding apparatus) faces a vacuum; his hands "l[ie] idly in his lap" (197). Unlike the Old Folks, however, what rushes in to fill the vacuum left by McTeague's loss of habit is rage—first at Marcus, later at Trina.

One of the first consequences of McTeague's loss of his profession is the need to give up the new habits that Trina has fostered: better beer, better tobacco, and clean cuffs. McTeague at first misses these comforts, but then suddenly slips "back into the old habits" of his pre-Trina days (209). Soon, however, this revised structure is undermined as well. Trina's miserliness and his own lack of resourcefulness make it increasingly impossible for McTeague to take stability for granted.

As the idea of Trina Sieppe, the withheld sexual object, disrupted McTeague's original structure of habit, so after the loss of economic stability, the idea of Trina the withholder of money disrupts the new, retrenched order. Thus passion, like obsessive preoccupation, is twice elicited in McTeague by what Trina withholds. Here, as elsewhere in the novel, deprivation spurs the self toward obsession and chaos.

The more McTeague "storms," the more tightly Trina draws the strings of her "little chamois-skin [money]-bag" (225). In turn, the more tightly Trina fastens her purse, the more McTeague comes to be obsessed with hatred of her, as once he was obsessed with desire. It is a kind of nightmarish distortion of the narrator's "conventional wisdom" about the "changeless order of things" in which "the man desir[es] the woman only for what she withholds" (62). With a kind of primordial ferocity suggestive of *Wuthering Heights,* loss is seen to stir passion, rage, and obsession in McTeague.

The crux at the end of the novel is McTeague's feeling of deprivation, not his lust for gold as such. McTeague feels that Trina is stealing what by right belongs to him. He experiences this withholding as an intolerable threat. Even as Trina feels threatened because of her intimacy with McTeague, so McTeague comes to feel undermined by his "submission" to Trina—especially to her ever-increasing stinginess.

Trina's niggardliness and her irritating presence together destroy McTeague's capacity to maintain even those habits on which he relied before his marriage. He can no longer afford steam beer, nor can he sit with his pipe undisturbed in his dental chair, "crop-full, stupid, and warm" (1). Thus, casting about for yet another stable structure, McTeague returns to the habits of his boyhood. He takes his fishing rod and retreats to the oceanfront, to pleasures long forgotten. Soon, taking Trina's money as he once "took" her love, he again frees himself from his preoccupation with Trina, by eliminating its source in what he sees as deprivation.

When McTeague, having spent the stolen money, returns to San Francisco, he constructs one more support system of routine. Working as a piano loader, he reestablishes his original Sunday habits as described in Chapter I. However, because Trina had pawned his concertina when he fled without it ". . . he could no longer play his six lugubrious airs . . . and it was a deprivation" (270). Fittingly, it is not merely Trina's withholding of money—or even of food—that goads McTeague to murder. McTeague decides to kill Trina when he finds his concertina in a pawn shop. Only then does McTeague's

> rage loom . . . big within him. His hatred of Trina came back upon him like a returning surge. He saw her small, prim mouth, her narrow blue eyes, her black mane of hair. (270)

In language that recalls McTeague's preoccupation with Trina, when he first desired her, McTeague is once again obsessed with Trina, obsessed now because of a loss that has undermined his sense of stability and pleasure, his reassuring frame of habit.[15]

Toward the end of the novel, McTeague again purges his obsessive rage—this time by murdering Trina—and proceeds to seek a sustaining structure of routine. After the murder, McTeague returns to the mines and to the occupation of his youth. "Within a week's time it seemed to him as though he had never been away" (282; compare 281). Repetition provides the illusion of control and stability; as in the case of Maria, it seems to freeze time and forestall change. However, automatistic repetition cannot provide effective control or stability. Just as Maria's habits ultimately do not protect her from implication in life processes, so McTeague's return to the mines cannot protect him from change and death. His return to his old ways for protection is as futile, and as telling, as the impulse that makes McTeague cling to his canary, even though it will hasten his undoing. Although, obviously, it is "an easy matter" (316) to track a man carrying a birdcage in the desert, McTeague's canary is part of the accustomed clothing of the self and, as such, is extremely difficult for him to part with.[16] McTeague's refusal to leave his canary behind is a measure of his inability to adapt, to change, and to make his peace with loss.

It is revealing to note in this context that what brings Trina and McTeague together in the first place is a tooth that Trina has broken. Trina cannot bear to contemplate losing a tooth; her refusal is adamant. It is just at this point that McTeague begins "to like her better and better" (18). In fact, McTeague soon energetically, and contrary to his customary procedure in such cases, engages in restoring rather than pulling the tooth, "[h]e could not say why" (19).

In his inarticulate, naively blundering way, McTeague abhors mutability; he craves wholeness and consistency, a soothing, stabilizing life of habit such as almost totally contents him at the start of the novel. From the first description of McTeague, a multitude of details underscores his lack of adaptability. But survival in the world of *McTeague,* not to mention satisfaction, is seen to depend precisely on the capacity to pivot, to adapt, to tolerate flux, self-exposure, spontaneous giving, and even enforced deprivation. Most of the characters of *McTeague* clearly lack this capacity and, encrusted with habit, are destroyed.

Indeed, the issue of adaptability as a criterion for survival is perhaps the one element of Darwinian thought that seems directly relevant to *McTeague,* as to *Vandover.* Despite the various statements of naturalist "philosophy" within the text, the question of adaptation itself is not placed in the foreground by the narrative voice of *McTeague.* Nonetheless, the characters in the novel are certainly marked by a crippling incapacity to adapt to change, and more particularly to loss.[17] It is as though Norris seized intuitively upon this aspect of naturalistic doctrine—the issue of adaptability—and incorporated it imaginatively into his vision without explicitly conceptualizing it. Ironically, it is the discursively formulated doctrinal material in the novel, the polemical statements about instinct and Chance, that resists integration into the governing structure of the text.

Perhaps Norris, at this stage of his career, still lacked the full courage of his creative imagination and drew back from confronting the issues that it raised. Perhaps the assertions of the narrative voice in *McTeague* even served a fortifying, defensive function for Norris, as characters within the novel rely upon their own particular repetitive systems for support. It is as if the naturalistic categories invoked by the narrative voice serve (like Maria's story or McTeague's song) as a kind of protective buffer—in this case, perhaps, against the full implications of a vision of chaos and of the extreme vulnerability of the self.

It is certain, however, that as Norris's career continues, his "naturalistic" formulations play an ever smaller role within his work. Other changes appear as well. After *McTeague,* compulsive behavior, like Maria's storytelling, is rarely perceived to be comic. Old Mr. Bessemer in *Blix* winds clocks, and Aunt Wess in *The Pit* counts church pews and light bulbs, but these are very minor comic figures, with little impact on other characters in the represented world of the text. In *The Octopus,* on the other hand, the measure of Magnus's defeat is his transformation into a kind of automaton, tying and untying piles of papers, arranging and rearranging them.

Moreover, after *McTeague,* rigid defensiveness, viewed as gravely problematic, regularly becomes characteristic of major figures; it becomes, in fact, a central imaginative crux. At the same time, other kinds of major characters begin to appear in Norris's works, characters who are capable of risking themselves. When Moran, like Maria Macapa, lowers her defenses and ventures into an intimate relationship, her own violent death soon follows. On the other hand, the Old Folks in *McTeague* may be seen as a paradigm for the process by which renunciation of defense safely leads to the expression of spontaneous feeling and gives rise in turn to loving human contact.

The story of Old Grannis and Miss Baker, however, is not just sentimental and grotesque; the "paradise" they achieve is a static one, where it is "always autumn" (242). Such a condition ultimately has much in common with their original state at the start of the novel. They now share their static world in mutual happiness, and this is an improvement. But the novels that follow *McTeague* cast a more critical eye on the implications of stasis as such and increasingly explore the potential value of renouncing both defensive structures and stasis in any form. Increasingly, value is seen to reside in the recognition of flux as the inevitable condition of life, with human contact and the creative imagination serving to alleviate the pain that inevitably accompanies such awareness.

5. The Language of Recovery: Word and Symbol in The Octopus

> The terror of sheer bigness grew slowly in her mind; loneliness beyond words gradually enveloped her.
>
> —Norris, *The Octopus*

> Annixter . . . [held] in deep respect the man who could rhyme words. . . . No doubt, there was not much use in poetry . . . [b]ut just the same, it . . . wasn't everyone who could rhyme "brave" and "glaive" and make sense out of it. Sure not.
>
> —Norris, *The Octopus*

In the years between his work on *McTeague* and *The Octopus,* Norris seems to have taken to heart William Dean Howells's comment, after reading *McTeague,* that the bright side of life has a legitimate place in literature.[1] Both *Blix* and *A Man's Woman* affirm many aspects of experience: love and marriage, change and self-knowledge, even the constructive potential of narrative. In the experience of Condy and Ward Bennett, writing becomes—no less than love—a catalyst for inner renewal.

Norris claimed that *The Octopus* signaled a return to "straight naturalism." Yet his "Epic of the Wheat" seems less a "going back . . . to the style of *McTeague*" (*Letters,* 48) than an experiment with a variety of narrative modes and a reexamination of issues that had preoccupied Norris even before *Vandover.* In *The Octopus* the vulnerable self, hard pressed in its bid for a measure of equilibrium, comes to the fore once again. But the tidy resolutions of *Blix* and *A Man's Woman* are now replaced by a more searching exploration of individual responses to the fear, rage, and powerlessness elicited by change and irreparable loss.

The opening scenes of *The Octopus* forcefully establish the treacherous nature of life within the represented world. That world is characterized by extreme instability, unpredictability, and brutality.[2] It is also one within which Norris's characters once again have the greatest difficulty accommodating to the vicissitudes of their experience.

In Chapter 1, Presley rapidly encounters a series of characters, each of whom conveys his own pieces of sudden bad news: Hooven is to be turned off Magnus's ranch after seven years of tenant farming; Harran has learned of the ranchers' defeat in their court dispute over freight rates for shipping wheat; Dyke has been fired by the railroad after ten years of steady work. Vanamee's story of sudden disaster is a tale of the past, but his "idyl," which was interrupted "with the abruptness of an explosion" (I, 35), remains an ever-present reality to him. This first chapter ends with the sudden intrusion of the noisy "crack passenger engine" upon "the beauty of [Presley's] poem"—another "idyl" (I, 46). Just when Presley thinks he is on the verge of grasping his "inspiration" (just when "the feeling of absolute peace and quiet and security and untroubled happiness and content seemed descending from the stars like a benediction") the single locomotive "shot by him with a roar, filling the air with . . . terrific clamor" (I, 46) and leaving in its wake a mass of slaughtered sheep.

Sudden devastation is what Norris's characters have feared and averted with varying degrees of success since *Vandover* and *McTeague*. But what had earlier been presented as an inner anxiety afflicting individual characters becomes generalized and objective in *The Octopus*—a defining characteristic of things as they are. Within the represented world of the novel, life is unstable, slippery, treacherous in the extreme. The central question explored by *The Octopus* could be put this way: How is one to live within such a deceptive, chaotic, untrustworthy world? The answer that emerges from the text cannot be fully accounted for by reference to evolutionary theism, laws of supply and demand, the benevolent power of love, or the emergence of good out of evil.[3]

On the whole, the central characters in the novel are seen to be unable or unwilling to accept life under the conditions that prevail. Both Presley and Vanamee, given to idylls, are obsessed from the outset with the galling limits of mortality and the insignificance of man himself. Such resolutions as they achieve are extremely problematic. Only through the story of Annixter, the third young "hero" of *The Octopus,* does the novel envision the possibility of transcending self-deception, chaos, fear, and loss.[4]

Unlike Presley and Vanamee, Annixter comes to accept both his own littleness and the possibility of loss. By the time of his sudden death, Annixter, alone within the world of *The Octopus,* has achieved a kind of inner balance, accepting life as a mysterious process that demands a certain humility. Annixter's own experience affords him plenty of opportunity to perceive the limits of individual power or control. But by the end of the novel, power is no longer a central issue for Annixter. The satisfactions of human contact begin to outweigh the dangers of risking oneself in relationships with others.

It is in the context of these issues that the symbol of the wheat acquires persuasive imaginative resonance. The cycle of the wheat serves within the world of *The Octopus* both as an instance of a natural process that (despite modern scientific technology) remains ultimately mysterious and as a process within which life and death are inextricably intertwined.

Father Sarria calls the wheat a "symbol of immortality" (I, 139). Annixter and Vanamee, in the course of their night vigils, come to see in the wheat a suggestion of spiritual rebirth and renewal. For Presley, the wheat is repeatedly identified with irrepressible force.[5] Yet no single character perceives the full implications of the meaning of the wheat. Within the structural framework of the text, the wheat suggests not merely force or renewal but perpetual change itself, process as such.

It has often been suggested that insofar as the image of the wheat connects with the story—the dramatic action—of the novel, Presley's final optimistic interpretation of life is inadequate. At the end of the novel, reflecting upon the wheat, Presley recalls Vanamee's words: that good comes out of evil, that death in one place means life in another. Presley's concluding optimism not only seems a facile conclusion to a complex and painful drama, it also violates the essential logic of the image of the wheat. The wheat cycle suggests not that evil in one place is balanced by good in another, but that death and birth are inextricably interrelated in a continuing organic cycle. Moreover the cycle—as cycle—exists in time, rather than space.

Father Sarria, to be sure, perceives the wheat as an image of renewal by seeing it as a process in time. But Father Sarria's interpretation is (like Presley's) misleading, because for Father Sarria, once "life" has followed death the cycle is complete. Like Annixter and Vanamee (and many critics of *The Octopus*), Father Sarria interprets the meaning of the wheat cycle by looking no further once renewal has occurred. Within *The Octopus,* however, it is clear that in the wheat field, as in the course of human events, death must inexorably (if not immediately) follow renewal. Indeed, even though many characters triumphantly affirm the rebirth of the wheat, it becomes clear as the novel continues that one can expect death to follow renewal much more reliably than one can expect renewal to follow death.[6] One can always depend on renewal as a possibility in nature, of course, but one cannot depend on it in any particular way. One does not know *when* the wheat will come up, nor even, in any specific season, *if* it will come up. When *The Octopus* opens, there have been two dry seasons; a third would mean ruin for the farmers, as Harran reflects (I, 54). In the event, unpredictably, the wheat comes up as a bumper crop—and ruin overtakes the farmers from another direction.

The image of the wheat thus functions in *The Octopus* as a powerful symbol of inevitable, unpredictable flux in nature and, by analogy, within the human world as well. *The Octopus* ends with Presley's vision of the force of the wheat as continuous production. But the novel opens with barren ground waiting to be plowed, and (despite the epiphanies of renewed life along the way) the novel closes after the harvest with barren ground progressively covering the San Joaquin again. Thus, the implicit "truth" is not only what Annixter and Vanamee discover during their night vigils—that renewal is possible in the self, as in nature; the truth is also that after renewed life, death is sure to reoccur—even as life, in one form or another, is sure to replace death in due course. This interrelatedness of life and death, however, is precisely what the characters in *The Octopus* cannot accept. Only Annixter becomes an exception to the rule.

Annixter experiences a kind of spiritual renewal in the course of the action. The process he undergoes may be understood on the analogy of the wheat once the wheat is perceived as an image of flux and change, an image of natural process that includes both renewal and the inevitability of death. Through the Annixter plot, the novel implies the possibility of being reconciled to the inevitably dynamic processes that govern human relations, as well as the life of the self.

It cannot be too strongly emphasized that the possibility of permanence is never envisioned as part of the life process. Many things are seen to be possible—indeed multiplicity and change are the only inevitable things—but nothing is seen to be possible in perpetuity. Permanence is precisely what one cannot expect in life. To insist upon permanence is (like Vanamee) to be mad.[7]

Thus, the problem of the individual self accepting the slipperiness of reality, integrating change, loss, and death, is central to *The Octopus*. While the problem is presented with greater dramatic immediacy than the solution, a solution is hinted at, both through the experience of Annixter and through the final encounter between Presley and Hilma.

The Octopus is an extremely sprawling, diffuse work—in many ways a "loose and baggy monster," as Henry James called *War and Peace*. Critics of the novel have often been baffled by its varied and contradictory stylistic levels. With its wide setting, its multiple actions, and its combination of disparate aesthetic modes, *The Octopus* certainly provides a sharp contrast to both *Vandover* and *McTeague*. If the underlying imaginative logic of *McTeague* lends itself to trim, sharp explication, an analysis of *The Octopus* necessarily involves less tidy formulations.

Norris's first two novels, moreover, center upon characters who are incapable of coping constructively with their experience. Only through the anomalous subplot of the Old Folks does *McTeague* suggest a potential ground of value. *The Octopus* not only takes up the negative concerns of the earlier work: questions of threat, loss, terror, and compulsive behavior. Through the figure of Presley, it also reengages another issue central to *Vandover*: the function of art within the psychic economy of the artist. Finally, in its treatment of the Annixter action, *The Octopus* complicates and extends the tenuous optimism projected through the minor figures of Old Grannis and Miss Baker in *McTeague*. I will now consider these issues in greater detail.

"'I hate a mystery,'" Hilma Tree explains to Annixter. "'I shouldn't like to think that anything could happen around me that I couldn't see or understand or explain'" (I, 161). Hilma, of course, is supremely naive. Her childlike innocence is repeatedly emphasized in the early chapters of *The Octopus*. But Hilma's view, simply stated, is typical of all the characters in the novel. Most of the characters could say, like Captain Ahab of *Moby-Dick,* "The inscrutable thing is chiefly what I hate."

Annixter's "scientific" preparations for farming are undertaken in an attempt to objectify and control the mysterious processes of nature. Vanamee's mystic invocation of his dead beloved is another version of the effort to conquer the unfathomable—in his case the ultimate mystery of death. Indeed, in the end, Vanamee believes he has done no less than prove "time was naught; change was naught. . . . Death was overcome" (II, 106).[8]

Dyke, Harran, Magnus Derrick, all struggle for control, at least of their own personal fates. The struggle for such mastery is inevitably doomed. By the end of the novel, Dyke has lost everything of value; Harran is dead; Magnus is a broken man, obsessively rearranging, tying, and untying piles of papers. His ranch is now owned by S. Behrman, whose imperious malevolence serves to reemphasize the treacherous and elusive nature of reality. Indeed, the extremely maddening effect of S. Behrman (and through him the railroad) on his opponents springs both from his utter imperturbability and from his devilish slipperiness. Nonetheless, by the end of the novel S. Behrman's own hold on life has been undone in its turn. Precisely when S. Behrman thinks he has become "Master of the wheat" (II, 324), the wheat itself destroys him.

The amount and quality of technology in the world of *The Octopus* would seem to make for at least a certain amount of control over nature. Annixter is not the only one who prepares "scientifically" for farming. Magnus's ranch is full of modern equipment; Harran takes infinite pains with his seed-wheat, keeping close watch over his instruments, maps, and ticker tape. Even S. Behrman takes pride in the technological ingenuity that has produced a grain elevator to streamline the process of transporting the wheat. Yet the wheat itself still maintains the prerogative typical of all forces and beings in the world of *The Octopus,* namely, ultimate unmanageability.

The wheat's de facto resistance to being fully controlled by human will is matched by its resistance to unambiguous interpretation.[9] Thus, while the wheat becomes an image of hope for Annixter and Vanamee, to Annie Derrick the wheat spells only terror; "so much wheat" stands for everything that Annie Derrick fears in this new, untamed environment, so different from that of her girlhood.

> [This] new order of things—a ranch bounded only by the horizons . . . where even when the land was resting, unploughed, unharrowed, and unsown, the wheat came up— troubled her, and even at times filled her with an undefinable terror. (I, 56–57)

Within the world of the novel, Annie Derrick is absolutely typical both in the reasons for and in the nature—if not in the particular object—of her fear. She feels helpless in the face of a vastness and a lack of control that render her totally impotent. Most of the other characters in the novel do not directly experience such terror, in part because they tend to be frenetically engaged in a struggle for control that is not the less absorbing because it turns out to be futile. Despite scientific farming, written agreements, and many new technological achievements (not the least of which is the railroad itself), "objective" reality remains so baffling that one cannot even recognize a dead man before one's eyes: the men who find Delaney's body in a field hold a long deliberation as to whether Delaney is dead or alive, without arriving at any consensus (II, 241–42).

The inner world is as difficult to control as the external world of events. Presley cannot find his "inspiration"; Magnus cannot decide on a course of action; Annixter cannot get Hilma Tree out of his mind. The feelings that Hilma elicits in Annixter are beyond his comprehension and his control. No wonder that he sits in a chair, after one bewildering early encounter, "staring fixedly at a thermometer on the wall" and recalling his "intention to buy a fine barometer, an instrument that could be accurately depended on" (I, 82).

The process that Annixter undergoes, in part through his relationship with Hilma, is much more interesting and complex than can be conveyed by the notion of redemption through love, or redemption of a man by a good woman. Annixter's character, at the outset, is perhaps best epitomized by his own name, which means, quite literally, one who says no. (If more proof were needed his first name is "Buck"!) Annixter says "no" on many occasions, just, it seems, for the sheer pleasure of it, or, like a small child, for the sense of his own power, as an assertion of his capacity to exercise control. Like a child, or like someone in a world largely resistant to willed intentions, Annixter is given to arbitrary and often contradictory self-assertions. Annixter's way of ending an argument is typical. His favorite, often-repeated phrase for this purpose—"maybe it is and then again maybe it isn't"—serves as a way out of every tight corner.

Annixter holds a number of dogmatic opinions, many of which are presented to the reader in Chapter 1 in a brief introductory background sketch. Interestingly, however, Annixter's contempt for doctors, Europeans, "feemales," and most people in general stands in marked contrast to his "deep respect [for] the man who could rhyme words" (I, 24).

Annixter's somewhat surprising respect for poets, which is one basis for his friendship with Presley, is less puzzling than it seems at first. Indeed, in a world where the individual's sphere of possible control is radically circumscribed, language appears to be one of the few areas where one can make order, impose some shape of one's own. Annixter, in fact, is acutely aware that even words are more slippery and harder to control than they seem; hence, the respect. "'It wasn't everyone,'" Annixter reflects, "'who could rhyme 'brave' and 'glaive,' and make sense out of it. Sure not'" (I, 24).

Annixter's respect for the mastery of words goes hand in hand with his underlying sense of the power of the word. When Annixter visits

Los Muertos looking for Magnus Derrick in Chapter 5, he encounters Annie Derrick and is immediately on his guard. "In an actual spasm of caution, he scarcely trusted himself to speak, terrified lest he should commit himself to something" (I, 175).

Annixter's terror of words as inordinately powerful is first revealed in the early sketch of his amorous involvement with a "timid little creature in a glove-cleaning establishment" (I, 25). Annixter develops this relationship with maximum caution. When he sends letters to the girl, he takes care neither to sign them nor to write them by hand. He makes carbons of these letters, which he files in his safe (one can't be too safe). Then suddenly, he breaks the whole thing off, reserving all the prerogatives of capriciousness for himself. "It was his only love affair. After that, he kept himself free. No petticoats should ever have a hold on him. Sure not" (I, 25).

It is no accident that Annixter's fear of being trapped by a petticoat should crystallize in the course of a written correspondence. Indeed, as the action of the novel unfolds, it becomes plain that Annixter's sense of the power and awesomeness of language is no more atypical than Annie Derrick's terror of uncontrolled vastness. To consider *The Octopus* in the light of this issue is to find that it is not only poets who use language as a wedge between the self and the threatening flow of chaotic pressures, both objective and subjective. Indeed, the issue of language itself is surprisingly central in a novel that seems to be primarily concerned with large natural and economic forces, set in the context of the great outdoors.

Obviously language has served man as a tool for survival ever since his emergence from the stone age. Philosophy and psychology, as well as evolutionary theory, made us familiar with the idea of language as an agent of control, long before structuralism and poststructuralism reversed the telescope to emphasize our imprisonment in language. Although Norris's work has never been considered in connection with such issues, *The Octopus* displays an extremely keen sense of the function of language, its pleasures and pitfalls, and it does so at many levels, both blatant and subtle.

The very plot of *The Octopus* depends largely on speeches and written material of various sorts: pamphlets, contracts, legal briefs, freight tariff listings. The conflict between the farmers and the railroad centers on the meaning of the original written pamphlets describing the conditions under which the farmers were to take possession of their land and the conditions under which they were "promised" the chance to buy it from the railroad at some future time. The climax of Book I takes place during Annixter's barn dance when Magnus reads the contents of a letter that has suddenly arrived from the railroad representatives fixing the value of the railroad land at a price that, from the ranchers' point of view, is a direct breach of promise and that "menaced [them all] with ruin" (I, 265).

The ranchers retire to Annixter's harness room where a meeting is held, resolutions drafted, and a League of Defense is formed. At the climax of this scene, Magnus stands hesitating, with "the pen in one hand, his wife's fingers in the other, the roll of signatures before him:

> The crowd surged forward roaring. Mrs. Derrick was swept back, pushed to one side . . . thrust to the wall. The throng of men, stamping, surrounded Magnus; she could no longer see him, but terror-struck, she listened. There was a moment's lull, then a vast thunder of savage jubilation. Magnus had signed. (I, 272)

The climax awaited by the roaring crowd is not the outcome of a gunfight, but the writing of a name. Like Annixter, making carbon copies of his unsigned love letters, the crowd is full of a kind of unexamined faith in, and implicit fear of, the power of the written word. There is certainly no agreement at this point as to just what the "League" stands for, or what it is intended to do.

The word itself, with its ostensibly binding capability, is one of the central weapons in the fight between the railroad and the farmers. Throughout the novel characters purposively try to protect themselves, to ensnare and/or destroy one another by means of the written (and sometimes spoken) word. A great deal of the action of *The Octopus* revolves around characters' conscious, purposive use of language as a medium of control: a way of creating a place for themselves within the treacherous world, destroying their opponents, creating bonds with others.

Within *The Octopus,* the plot gives prominence to the coercive power of language as such. By publishing a newspaper account of

"Magnus Derrick's 'deal' with the political bosses" (II, 266), Genslinger first blackmails Magnus and then, breaking his promise, destroys him. The railroad's own view of the power of words is clearly revealed when it stops all railway traffic after the fight at the ditch. As Presley puts it, "Not a single local train was running [no mail moved, no telegrams were sent] except those emanating from railway officials. The story of the fight . . . was to be told to San Francisco and the outside world by S. Behrman, Ruggles, and the local P. and S. W. agents" (II, 251).

Furthermore, the many written and spoken agreements in *The Octopus* utterly fail either to stabilize relationships or to neutralize threats. In fact, broken trust is one of the central issues of the novel. True to his name at least, Lyman goes back on his word to the ranchers. When Annixter's home is seized, the Leaguers fail to honor their pledges to one another. Genslinger breaks his promise to Magnus after pocketing his hush money. In addition, Magnus's own sense of failure crystallizes with the awareness of not being believed, of being thought a liar (II, 268–69). Presley experiences a similar sense of failure after his Opera House speech, when he feels he has "not once held the hearts of his audience" (II, 262). In this context it is not surprising to find that the (wholly private) relationship between Annixter and Hilma comes to a climax when Annixter realizes with astonishment that despite, or because of, all that has passed between them, Hilma *trusts* him. As Annixter states in amazement, she accepts his "spoken word" (II, 119).

Insofar as struggles for stability and power (as well as issues of trust) take shape through contracts, letters, legal writs, newspaper stories, and so on, they involve the characters' deliberate use of language as a means of control, aggression, or self-protection. Still more interesting, however, is the way individual characters use language quite unconsciously for analogous purposes. Despite the slightly Wild West atmosphere of *The Octopus,* language seems to be the most readily available weapon, used by virtually every character in the novel for unwitting purposes of self-defense and self-definition. (Genslinger is not a gunslinger but a newspaperman.) Nearly every character regularly finds occasion to seek stability or self-protection through words, sometimes a phrase or two, sometimes a story, very often arranged in some repetitive pattern.

Presley is the most obvious example of a character engaged in a struggle for existence through the word. "'[W]hy write?'" Vanamee asks him at one point, contemplating "the heat of the desert, the glory of the sunset, the blue haze of the mesa"—in short, the West itself. "'Why not *live* in it?'" Presley answers Vanamee without hesitation: "'I could not lose myself like that in your desert.'" It is as if to lose himself in this sense, especially in someone else's territory, would be quite literally to lose his self, his being, altogether. Presley's writing, from his own point of view, directly protects him from such danger. If he could not "find expression," he would, as he says, "suffocate" (I, 39), stripped of the means for self-defense.

For other characters, literature clearly serves a similar function, not as output but as input. Annie Derrick is firmly entrenched in a fortress of literary works from the past. "Her taste was of the delicacy of point lace" (I, 57). The order and form of Walter Pater, Tennyson, "the flaccid banalities of the 'Minor Poets'" (I, 57), seem to protect her from being engulfed by that untamed vastness where wheat grows as far as the eye can see, even without benefit of cultivation. Annixter, too, has his literary shelter at the beginning of the novel. His interminable rereading of *David Copperfield,* though it perhaps reflects a more vigorous taste than Anne Derrick's, serves a similar function, providing a secure retreat from stress. Moreover, to take an example previously cited in another context, Annixter's two recurrent verbal formulas—"sure not," and "maybe it is and then again maybe it isn't"—both serve a self-protective, stabilizing function that is absolutely typical within the world of *The Octopus* and, indeed, throughout Norris's work.

In *The Octopus,* as in the earlier fiction, such defensive behavior is generally elicited by a threat that is obscure in its nature and source. The exasperating refusal of S. Behrman and the railroad representatives in general to define their terms and show their cards is typical of all the threatening (and especially climactic) events in the novel.[10] Obscurity is compounded by surprise. The barn dance at the end of Book I is twice interrupted by potential disaster, each time with the effect of a sudden thunderstorm. The fight at the ditch takes place with a similar effect. "'We have been taken by surprise, gentlemen, after all,'" as Magnus says; "'totally off our guard'" (II, 220).

Throughout *The Octopus,* such "bolts out of the blue" elicit immediate verbal responses, but the novel also provides many examples of the process by which verbal structures come to contain rage, fear, and anxiety. Within *The Octopus,* language and narrative appear most effective in dealing with terror or loss that has already been experienced. Moreover, it would seem that the more devastating an experience, the more totally its narrative rendering usurps the emotional present of the character, and the more elaborately wrought the narrative itself tends to be.

Repeated words may, of course, serve merely passing needs—for containment, control, or deflection of painful and embarrassing feelings. When Annixter barges into Ruggles's office with his checkbook, trying to force Ruggles to name his price and finalize the sale of land, Ruggles refuses:

> Annixter stormed out of the room, slamming the door behind him, and Ruggles, trembling with anger, turned to his desk and to the blotting pad written all over with the words Lands, Twenty dollars, Two and a half, Option, and over and over again, with great swelling curves and flourishes, *Railroad, Railroad, Railroad.* (I, 190)

By repeatedly writing the word *railroad* on his blotting pad, Ruggles finds a convenient outlet for his seething rage at Annixter. Since Ruggles' encounter with Annixter is not of central importance in his personal experience, a little stabilizing repetition would seem to go a long way.

More elaborate defensive verbal strategies figure in other brief scenes. Early in the novel, Annixter finds himself uncomfortably embarrassed in the presence of Hilma, who is unselfconsciously bringing him his supper. Suddenly he begins to talk about the dog who sometimes wandered into his house: "He could not let the subject rest. For no reason that he could explain even to himself, he recurred to it continually" (I, 81). As in the case of Ruggles, the particular source of Annixter's agitation is temporary and requires only a temporary defensive ploy.

Elsewhere in the novel, storytelling on a larger scale serves a more elaborate function. In *The Octopus,* more consistently than in Norris's earlier works, storytelling is presented as an extremely common, spontaneous human response in times of crisis, and particularly after a crisis. In the aftermath of the gunfight between Delaney and Annixter,

> [o]n all sides the reminiscences began to circulate. At least one man in every three had been involved in a gunfight at some time of his life. "Ah, you ought to have seen in Yuba County one time—" "Why, in Butte County in the early days—" "Pshaw! this to-night wasn't anything! Why once in a saloon in Arizona, when I was there—" and so on, over and over again. . . . Even the women recalled terrible scenes. . . . Stories by the hundreds went the round of the company. (I, 255)

It would appear that memory, which in *Vandover and the Brute* failed to contribute to coherence in Vandover's understanding of "the story of his life," very often does serve to provide precisely that: memory can function as a kind of reservoir in which episodes from the individual past are kept on tap ready to come to the aid of the self when present experience becomes especially chaotic. Faced with a present threat to the coherence of the self, faced with loss of accustomed order (whether internal or external), the self tends to find comfort in the testimony of past experiences preserved and ordered in memory and retold in words.

A fascinating "slip" in the text of the novel provides more proof that such a notion is absolutely basic in Norris's work and close to the center of his creative enterprise in *The Octopus.* "Stories by the hundreds" are passed around Annixter's barn after his fight with Delaney. It is Annixter himself, however, who is pivotal within this episode. For him the incident is important in a number of ways, especially because of his sudden awareness of Hilma's love for him, as reflected in her eyes when danger threatens.

> Long after, Annixter could recall this moment. *For years* he could with but little effort reconstruct the scene—the densely packed crowd flattened against the sides of the barn . . . the mingled smell of evergreens, new wood, sachets and powder smoke; the . . . squealing of the buckskin, the uneven explosions of the revolvers . . . and in the open space in the center

> of the floor, himself and Delaney, maneuvering swiftly in a cloud of smoke. (I, 253, my emphasis)

If my argument has been persuasive, the emphasis, at such a crucial juncture, on memory preserving a moment for years might seem almost predictable. Yet Annixter is dead by the end of the book, dead less than a year after the fight with Delaney. Such an oversight on Norris's part must be taken, I believe, as a measure of the importance he attached to the role of memory in ordering and synthesizing experience. Memory, shaped in language, appears to be full of both destructive and constructive potential; it is clearly the tool most readily available for anyone in crisis, and especially after a crisis.

Norris's obsessive storytellers are generally introduced to the reader with their habits fully formed. In *The Octopus* Caraher, retelling the story of his wife's death "by the railroad," is yet another such character. *The Octopus,* however, provides a variety of additional perspectives on both the genesis and the function of repetitive phrases and stories. The experience of Dyke clearly illustrates the process through which a fixed story comes to serve its protective function.

Dyke's financial and moral ruin occurs when he discovers that the freight rates for shipping hops have been raised and that, therefore, he will not be able to pay the debts incurred in the course of raising his first crop. His initial reaction is rage, the furious impulse to resist devastation. However, he soon realizes the impossibility of resistance, and the impulse to fight destruction is replaced by the impulse to render the experience in words. On the way home from Bonneville, Dyke tells Caraher his story:

> For the fiftieth time Dyke told the story. Already it had crystallized into a certain form. He used the same phrases with each repetition, the same sentences, the same words. In his mind it became set. Thus he would tell it to anyone who would listen from now on, week after week, year after year, all the rest of his life. (II, 70)

For Dyke, then, life is reduced to the memory of his most devastating experience. The repetitive narrative is the measure of his impotence. Control of his experience, his immediate surroundings, his ultimate fate has been beyond him, but at least he can "crystallize" his story "into a certain form," letting it "set" in his mind.[11] His experience, fossilized in narrative, no longer stirs rage and anxiety. However, it has become the tombstone on Dyke's present as well as his future.

Annixter's experience, unique within *The Octopus* (and rare in Norris's fiction altogether), is, as I have suggested, the diametrical opposite of this process—a progressive opening up to experience rather than a narrowing and fixing. Annixter's relationship with Hilma, his growing ability to tolerate the give and take of love and of human contact altogether, frees him from the defensive strategies behind which he hides at the start of the novel. After he has reached an understanding with Hilma, we hear only once more of his reading *David Copperfield*.[12] His own repetitive verbal formulas no longer recur at all. In fact, Annixter has come so far from reliance upon these formulas that Presley can joke with him about them (II, 178). They are no longer adequate or necessary in his relation to experience.

Annixter's readiness to expose himself to others and to experience itself without his insulating armor reaches its climax in his proposal to Hilma. When Annixter asks Hilma to marry him, he dwells on what he had learned during his all-night vigil:

> I know what love means now, and instead of being ashamed of it, I'm proud of it. If I never was to see you again I would be glad I've lived through that night just the same. (II, 117–18)

Annixter here speaks for the sustaining power and value of love, contained as experience by the self and of benefit to the self as experience, quite apart from Annixter's actual fate in relation to his object of desire. His experience is meaningful to Annixter at this point, whether or not Hilma marries him, even if he were never to see her again. This is love that (unlike Vanamee's) authentically nullifies the crippling power of loss, love that is above or beyond mutability precisely because it accepts the ever-present possibility of change and disappointment.

Paradoxically, Vanamee's absolute refusal to accept change and death as a part of his relationship with Angèle makes his obsessive memory of the past a testament to the inordinate power of mutability and loss, rather than a victory over change and death as Vanamee himself would have it. Indeed, Vanamee's impulse toward transcendence becomes a kind of parody of itself as his experience unfolds in the course of the novel. It is not rude, earthy Annixter but Vanamee, the mystic, who needs fleshly proof of eternity. And even while Vanamee's "undying love" accepts the interchangeability of individual objects, it ultimately demands (and obsessively depends on) the presence of the physical object itself. In contrast, Annixter's love, at least in principle, includes the possibility of integrating loss, with the aid of memory. ("'If I never was to see you again, I would be glad I've lived through that night just the same,'" as Annixter says.)

Of course it is Hilma, not Annixter, who is put to the test. After Annixter dies, Hilma is left to face the problem of sustaining loss and yet proceeding with life. When Presley encounters Hilma at the end of the novel she is in mourning and her mourning defines her. Indeed, she would seem to be well on her way to becoming an obsessive mourner, à la Vanamee. Pale, stark, dressed in black, Hilma's appearance underwrites her words as she tells Presley that her life has had meaning only since her relationship with Annixter and can only have meaning through his memory now that he is dead. "'I would rather be unhappy in remembering [Annixter],'" Hilma says, "'than happy in forgetting him'" (II, 339).

The final image of Hilma epitomizes the greatest danger in the world of *The Octopus*: rigid resistance to the ebb and flow of life, the flux of experience kept at bay with the aid of implacable memory. If Hilma were to proceed in the direction she seems to be taking, her preoccupation with the past would, like that of Vanamee, Caraher, Dyke, Maria Macapa, or the sea captain in *Blix,* effectively annihilate the possibility of inner process, development, and renewal of any kind.

Presley, however, suggests to Hilma that she could look at her situation from another point of view. His words open another frail option to her, an alternative to self-insulation and arrested development. "'The part of you that belonged to your husband can always keep him sacred,'" Presley says.

> "[T]hat part of you belongs to him and he to it. But you are young; you have all your life to live yet. Your sorrow need not be a burden to you. If you consider it as you should—as you will some day, believe me—it will

> only be a great help to you. It will make you more noble, a truer woman, more generous." (II, 339)

Presley's advice offers only a thread of hope; but it points to a potential life line: the possibility of confronting death yet going on with life, denying neither life nor death in the process. Seen in this light, memory need not necessarily put an end to every possibility of ongoing experience. It can, on the contrary, contribute to a dynamic, evolving self—as it begins to do for Annixter before his death.[13]

Presley's sense of memory as a potentially constructive force within the self becomes a central issue in *The Pit*. Within *The Octopus* it is dramatized as the wasted potential of Annixter and articulated as Presley's counsel. Norris's choice of Presley as the spokesman for this view involves a certain irony, to be sure. Unlike Annixter, Presley himself tries to run away from both life and death, finding their stubborn interrelatedness intolerable and taking refuge at last in Vanamee's notion that in the long run there will be a happy balance between good and evil. Still, the most authentic note of optimism at the end of the novel is Presley's suggestion to Hilma that individual experience can proceed despite inevitable periods of arrest and even near devastation. Presley's words imply that under certain conditions the individual self—like the wheat—may be capable of renewal, generating greater or richer life by integrating the experience of death.

The Octopus is pervaded by the romantic notion of the self as unfolding, developing, dynamically in process. But even as the growth of the wheat may itself be arrested, so the growth of the individual is seen to be far from simple or inevitable. The narrative voice speaks specifically of Annixter's "arrested development" at one point (II, 210), and the idea of arrested development is surely applicable to Vanamee, "whose life had suddenly stopped at a certain moment of its development" (I, 32). The early images of Annie Derrick (with her youthful appearance and her look of "innocence, such as one might expect to see in a young girl," I, 55), like the final images of Dyke, Hilma, and Presley, all serve as reminders of the myriad obstacles to individual growth in an unstable and threatening world.

Much of the power of *The Octopus* stems from its capacity to project a sense of flux, change, constant process that frames the events of the main action: birth and death, birth and death again, in constant alteration.[14] The dramatic force of the novel derives from the struggle of individual characters with vital processes beyond their control. Defensive strategies, usually based on repetitive behavior, are a common by-product of such struggle throughout Norris's fiction. *McTeague,* as we have seen, is pervaded by repetitive activities of many kinds. *The Octopus,* however, not only projects an elaborate vision of the teleology of such strategies but, particularly through the experience of Annixter, it also dramatizes the sublime and painful possibility of living life without them.

In a sense, Presley's advice to Hilma could be taken as an epigraph for the novel as a whole. His romantic affirmation, however, is easier said than done. The text surely does not demonstrate the value, to Presley himself, of his own encounters with pain and death. Norris's portrait of Presley offers no model for the value of suffering, or the integration of experience into the self. Indeed, Presley appears to possess virtually no "self" of his own. He sustains no ideological position, no conviction, no emotion for long. He himself speaks of his impulses as being "abrupt and of short duration" (II, 359, 360). In this sense he is at the opposite pole from Vanamee, who is irredeemably stuck in one moment of time. Midway between Vanamee and Presley, however, stands Annixter, and potentially Hilma, engaged in the effort to retain a human shape amid the flux of life and death.

Like many of Norris's characters—perhaps like the "boy Zola" in Norris himself—Presley attempts to counter flux with his own written words and with philosophic abstractions. Toward the end of the novel, disillusioned by his own creative gift, by the ineffectiveness of his shaping and ordering verbal powers, he turns to formulations provided by others—Caraher, Shelgrim, Vanamee. Presley is tempted in turn by political, economic, and philosophical rhetoric, but none of these affords him either stability or inner strength.

Even in his final encounter with Hilma, when Presley feels his "tired heart" reaching "out toward her," the human impulse is immediately transformed into "a longing to give the best that was in him *to the memory of her*" (II, 338, my emphasis). Presley's impulse, at this juncture, is to "reshape his purposeless, half-wasted life" by taking "the memory of [Hilma] . . . for his inspiration" (II, 338). Thus, at the end of the book Presley has come full circle. Still seeking "inspiration," he now hopes to find it in a living woman whom he can turn into "a memory" even while she stands before him. It is a kind of inversion of the end of *Blix*: Presley, unlike Condy, cannot renounce the safety of fixed images and personal isolation.[15]

Presley's own "arrested development" is comically reemphasized by the last extended conversation recorded in the text—Presley's leave-taking from the entrepreneur Cedarquist. "'Good-bye, sir'" says Presley, at the end of an exchange that has alluded to the famine in India.

> "Get fat yourself while you're about it, Presley," [Cedarquist] observed, as the two stood up and shook hands.
>
> "There shouldn't be any lack of food on a wheat ship. Bread enough, surely."
>
> "Little monotonous, though. 'Man cannot live by bread alone.'" (II, 357)

Cedarquist's advice notwithstanding, Presley (like many characters in Norris's works) seems virtually incapable of varying his diet.[16]

We recall that obsessive storytellers throughout Norris's fiction stultify inner process, present and future, by repeatedly reliving a past moment in memory and speech. In Presley a preoccupation with words and aesthetic form takes the place of spontaneous feeling and lasting personal commitment. In the course of the novel, Presley responds to his experience with some vehemence; he struggles valiantly to transform his inchoate responses into language and art. Yet, like Vandover, Presley ultimately fails to turn his artistic gift into either an effective medium of expression or a vehicle of stabilizing form. Poetry, prose, memory, consciousness, none of these enable Presley either to escape or to express the events, or the feelings, that threaten him with chaos and "suffocation."

While Presley councils Hilma to remember *as well as* to forget, he himself finally turns his back not only on his recent experience but on the possibility of human contact as suggested by Hilma, and on his effort to write as well. Thus, Presley's final advice to Annixter's widow may seem meaningful to her and is supported by the logic of the novel as a whole. But for Presley to put his idea into words is to remove it from the reality of his own experience.

We have seen that Vanamee, at the start of the novel, argues against Presley's tendency to "write" rather than "live," as if contemplating an either/or proposition. At the end of the novel, Presley indeed can do neither. As for Vanamee himself, he eschews words specifically, refusing to "tell" his idyl to Presley at all (II, 345). Only Annixter's vision can be both translated into words, however gropingly (I, 117–18; II, 180), and also integrated into the ongoing life of a potentially resilient, experiencing self.

For Presley ("a poet by training") as for Vanamee ("a poet by instinct"), the uneasy relationship between art and life remains unresolved and becomes instead a dichotomy. Only Annixter, with his surprising admiration for poets, his growing humility and dawning acceptance of others, ultimately displays the capacity to give "his imagination full play" (II, 81) while nonetheless remaining in touch with the events and the people around him.

Like Keats, who could wish for "a life of sensations rather than of thoughts," Norris often spoke of the value of "life" over "literature."[17] Yet "life" and "literature" were not for Norris, as they were for Presley or Vanamee, mutually exclusive possibilities. Not only was literature, quite obviously, a vital part of Norris's own life, but Norris's work (like Keats's) contains an extremely subtle and elaborate vision of the shifting relationship between experience and words, life in "reality" and life as transformed through memory and art.

Clearly Norris himself was committed to filling his fiction with as much "real" life as he could verify, document, and represent in words. The amount of researched reality informing Norris's work may have been partly responsible for obscuring the nature of Norris's achievement in transforming documented facts into the art of fiction. Again, Norris's emphasis on telling your "yarn" and letting style "go to the devil" has also helped to obscure the fact that much of his fiction, while apparently grounded in objective "reality," is nonetheless engaged in a vital exploration of the relationship between the reality being explored and the medium of exploration: words, memory, and the storytelling impulse.

Certainly *The Octopus* has never been seen to approach any of these issues, except partially through the figure of Presley, the declared writer who has a problem both with writing and with living.

While Norris's portrait of Presley surely dramatizes the crippling possibilities of writing as defense, we have seen how the text also explores other uses of language, both for better and for worse. The vitality of *The Octopus* is derived, at least in part, from its bewildering variety of indirect approaches to the question of how reading, writing, storytelling and memory may serve, or fail, to protect the self from uncontrolled vastness, within and without, and from the irrepressible flux of life itself.

6. Coming of Age in The Pit

"Oh, why limit one's absorption to business?" replied Corthell, sipping his wine. "'Is it right for one to be absorbed 'altogether' in anything—even in art, even in religion?"

—Norris's *The Pit*

"That's not poetry, maybe, but it's the truth."

—Jadwin in Norris's *The Pit*

"I'm just going to live . . . and oh, honey, how I will dress the part!"

—Laura in Norris's *The Pit*

When it first appeared, *The Pit* was a considerable popular success.[1] Since then its power to attract both the critic and the general reader has significantly diminished. There is little doubt that the imaginative vitality of *The Pit* cannot compare with that of either *McTeague* or *The Octopus,* and the image of the Pit itself has seemed sterile, perhaps the most sterile of Norris's governing images. Unlike the gold in *McTeague* or the wheat in *The Octopus,* the image of the Pit has not attracted the critical attention it deserves.[2]

While Norris's last novel surely has failings, the image of the Pit does not seem to me one of them. On the contrary, the Pit is among the most vital symbols in Norris's work. With its several literal meanings, the Pit provides a backdrop against which the dramatic action of the novel unfolds and a conceit that refracts and elucidates the central concerns of the text.

As we have seen, the pivotal issues in Norris's earlier work are often obscured by misleading statements of "naturalistic" philosophy. Sometimes the imaginative center of a novel is most boldly articulated through a minor character whose relevance to the main action is less than obvious. At the same time, sordid plot developments that may appear to contradict one another have, for decades, monopolized the attention of Norris's readers.

None of these problems arises in connection with *The Pit.* Discursive statements by the narrative voice have virtually disappeared. Subplots or subsidiary characters and events are kept to a minimum. The critical issue most often addressed by readers of *The Pit* has been, first, the relationship of the business plot to the love plot and, second, the meaning and effectiveness of the pat, even moralistic, ending.[3]

I would suggest that despite its weaknesses (the ending among them) *The Pit* is conceptually still richer than Norris's earlier works. Moreover, the issues with which *The Pit* is directly concerned are those that, in my view, consistently (if sometimes obliquely), inform Norris's fiction from the start. The questions at issue are these: On what basis is it possible to integrate, stabilize, realize the self? How is one's present self constituted, and how is it related to one's past self, or selves? What defensive strategies may be used by the self in its quest for equilibrium? What is the price of defense? What is the ground, and the price, of freedom from defense? These issues are both conceptually and dramatically central in *The Pit.* Moreover, they are explored with a cogency, subtlety, and complexity unrivaled in Norris's earlier works.

The style or method of *The Pit* indicates another new departure for Norris. While *The Octopus* rendered a space and a population so wide that Norris was impelled to include both a map of the "territory" and a list of characters at the beginning of his text, *The Pit* is concerned with only a handful of characters and a few indoor settings. These characters and settings are explored with increasing intensity and embedded in a web of allusive references that pervades the whole novel and further distinguishes it from Norris's previous fiction. In *The Pit* the implications of the action are most effectively elucidated by attention to the wide range of literary and cultural associations informing the text throughout.[4]

The image of the Pit itself provides a convenient starting point. The Chicago Wheat Pit, the pit of the theater and, potentially, the pit of hell, provide both literal and figurative contexts within which the central issues of the novel are explored. Among the literal contexts, of course, the Wheat Pit is dominant. It is the dynamic operation of the Wheat Pit that comes to provide both the climax of the action and an image for the inner dialectic of the self.

The Wheat Pit may be taken, first of all, as the ground upon which both Jadwin and Laura struggle for a form through which to affirm and stabilize themselves. For Jadwin, obviously, the Pit—the actual, literal Wheat Pit at the Board of Trade—becomes the arena within which he tests his capacity to predict and impose his will upon the future price of wheat. He would second-guess and dominate "the very Earth itself" (374) and by so doing would assert the incomparable superiority of his knowledge, his clarity of vision, and his capacity to exercise control over men and events.

Laura's search for "herself" or for self-affirmation in the context of the Pit goes far beyond her obvious struggle to extricate Jadwin from his own involvement there. But in order to perceive the full implications of Laura's personal struggle in and through the Pit, we must also perceive the Wheat Pit as a kind of stage. The text repeatedly underscores this connection, amplifying it with reference to Laura's general propensity for theatrics.

Norris himself considered Laura's character to be the structural and thematic center of *The Pit*.[5] A host of images, literary allusions, internal monologues, and other devices certainly give prominence to her "inner" dialectic. Yet Laura sometimes seems a peculiarly blank, even lifeless, creation, the various elements of which ultimately fail to cohere. The problem of coherence, however, is imaginatively central within the text, and despite its failings, the characterization of Laura directly addresses this issue.

Laura's histrionic talent is a major element in the depiction of her struggle for self-definition. It is partly with reference to her "grand manner" that Laura is introduced to the reader, and to Jadwin, in the first chapter of the novel (14). After her marriage to Jadwin, it is by virtue of "her 'grand manner'" that, "pos[ing] a little," she seems to find "the solution of the incongruity between herself—the Laura of moderate means and quiet life—and the massive luxury with which she [is] . . . surrounded" (213). Ultimately, however, the depiction of

Laura fails to resolve the repeatedly noted contradictions in her character.[6] Laura's histrionic gift, far from leading to a synthesis of warring elements within her, merely dramatizes the virtually insoluble problem of how to tell "the dancer from the dance."

"'It's myself, for the moment, whatever it is'" (312), Laura says when Jadwin reacts with confusion to her rendering of Theodora, Athalia, and Carmen in turn. The distinction between the dramatized roles, and the "self" within or beneath, is even more elusive when Laura, speaking to Corthell of her childhood, begins "by dramatising," but soon finds herself

> acting—acting with all her histrionic power at fullest stretch, acting the part of a woman unhappy amid luxuries. . . . Her voice was the voice of Phèdre, and the gesture of lassitude with which she let her arms fall into her lap was precisely that which only the day before she had used to accompany Portia's plaint of—my little body is a-weary of this great world.
>
> Yet at the same time, Laura knew that her heart was genuinely aching with real sadness, and that the tears which stood in her eyes were as sincere as any she had ever shed. (294–95)

Laura's self-dramatization gains additional meaning through the text's association of the Wheat Pit with theater. Not only do theaters usually have a "pit" in front of the stage, but the idea of a theater pervades the novel's final chapter, within which Jadwin's financial ruin takes place. The last chapter, Chapter X, begins by echoing, most explicitly, the atmosphere of the opera scene with which the novel begins. Specific parallels between the two scenes include the dense crowds that severely hinder movement in both auditoriums (5, 381); the "rows of theater chairs" in the Pit itself (385); the gong that marks the start of trading, and the little electric bell in the theater (25); the scraps of random financial conversation in both audiences; the applause and cheering of the crowd that, after each respective climax, momentarily drowns out all other sounds (23, 395); and the program sellers who sell "'Books of the opera. Words and music of the opera'" (33) and the newsboys who, after Jadwin's "final exit . . . from the scene of his many victories" (396), call out "'Extra . . . extra! All About the Smash of the Great Wheat Corner! . . . the Failure of Curtis Jadwin'" (412).

The final chapter of *The Pit* renders the climax of two separate but related dramas—direct analogues of the two dramas enacted in the opera scene of Chapter I. When the novel begins, Jadwin and Laura are part of a theater party that has come to watch the opera *Faust*.[7] Laura, in particular, is mesmerized by the stage, though she follows what is going on with difficulty. In addition, intermittent background talk within the audience interferes with Laura's pleasure. Talk of the latest financial debacle—the Helmick failure—repeatedly intrudes a "discordant element" (22) upon what Laura experiences as "all the harmony of the moment" (23)—a disjunction reminiscent of Presley's irritation at the "immovable facts" that intrude upon his "grand scheme of harmony" in the first chapter of *The Octopus*.

Laura's own "love scene" with Sheldon Corthell occupies her during the first intermission: "[H]is low voice was . . . in a way a mere continuation of the duet just finished" (23). In the next intermission, a conversation with Jadwin gives Laura a keen sense of "that other drama . . . working itself out close at hand, . . . equally romantic, equally passionate, but . . . real, actual, modern"—the drama of commerce in the city (34). Laura returns to her seat somewhat abstracted, and "the last act of the opera did not wholly absorb her attention" (35). Indeed, the last act of the opera receives no further mention in Chapter I, although the earlier scenes are described in detail, complete with lines cited and attributed to particular performers.

The final chapter of *The Pit,* however, may be seen as a revised version of the last act of *Faust,* neglected by Laura (as by the text itself) in Chapter I. The last chapter of *The Pit* is composed of the same materials as the first, with a redistribution of emphases. In Chapter X the drama enacted in the Wheat Pit is no longer on the margins; it is the drama of Jadwin's own financial ruin, a drama that must have a major effect on Laura, even though she is still not "wholly absorbed" by its unfolding events, as Page angrily charges (399–400). The climax, when Jadwin's "corner" breaks, leads directly to the final scene of Chapter X, in which Jadwin's eleventh-hour return home saves Laura from fleeing with Corthell to perdition.

Significantly, the scene in which Jadwin "saves" Laura (almost at the very moment that Corthell prepares to claim her for himself) is unmistakably reminiscent of *Faust,* where Marguerite is taken off to heaven just as Mephistopheles pronounces her to be lost. Indeed, Laura literally conceives of her Corthell-temptation in terms of a pit of hell, "black and without bottom" (360). This notion is reinforced by not one but two hells in Sheldon Corthell's name.

Throughout *The Pit* Laura is poised between Jadwin and Corthell. Yet what her conflict signifies is not self-evident. The polarity is far more complex than that of the artist versus the businessman, and the image of the Pit can serve to clarify the issues. It becomes easier to define what Corthell represents once we understand the image of Jadwin projected through his relation to the Pit.

In Chapter III the narrative voice says that Jadwin,

> unimaginative though he was, had long since conceived the notion of some great, some resistless force within the Board of Trade Building that held the tide of the streets within its grip, . . . there, a great whirlpool, a pit of roaring waters spun and thundered, sucking in the life tides of the city . . . then vomiting them forth again. (79)

Intermittent passages throughout the novel elaborate Jadwin's notion of the Pit as a "resistless force," "a pit of roaring waters," a "whirlpool" of constant flux with the primordial power of "creation itself" (387). Jadwin's notion of subduing all this "by the might of his single arm" (392) is one of the central motives for his involvement in the Pit (compare 80). Jadwin does in fact succeed, for a time, in predicting the course and controlling the flow of the wheat, despite its

> infinite immeasurable power . . . its roar, . . . the chaff and dust of its whirlwind passage . . . coeval with the earthquake and glacier, . . . a primal basic throe of creation itself, unassailable, inviolate, and untamed. (387; compare 80).

While the repeated descriptions of the wheat and the Board of Trade unmistakably recall descriptive passages in Zola's *Germinal,* Norris's evocation of the wheat suggests another allusion that has so far gone unnoted. The terms used for the wheat in *The Pit* are so reminiscent of Coleridge's "Kubla Khan" that the connection cannot be fortuitous. Like Kubla Khan, whose "stately pleasure dome" is poised upon a "deep . . . chasm," "[W]here Alph the sacred river ran / Through caverns measureless to man," Jadwin imposes a precarious order of his own upon chaos, laying "his puny human grasp upon Creation" (374). Jadwin's structure—his "corner"—like Kubla Khan's pleasure dome, straddles the "slipping and sliding of some almighty and chaotic power" (373). The following lines from Coleridge's poem suggest the charged environment of the "pleasure dome":

> But oh! that deep romantic chasm which slanted
> Down the green hill athwart a cedarn cover!
> . . . .
> And from this chasm, with ceaseless turmoil seething,
> As if this earth in fast thick pants were breathing,
> A mighty fountain momently was forced:
> Huge fragments vaulted like rebounding hail,
> Or chaffy grain beneath the thresher's flail:
> And 'mid these dancing rocks at once and ever
> It flung up momently the sacred river.
> Five miles meandering with a mazy motion
> Through wood and dale the sacred river ran,
> Then reached the caverns measureless to man,
> And sank in tumult to a lifeless ocean. (lines 17–28)

The relevance of "Kubla Khan" to Jadwin's struggle goes far beyond the poem's specific reference to "chaffy grain beneath the thresher's flail" or the earth breathing "in fast thick pants," phrases already echoed in the plowing scenes of *The Octopus*.

Jadwin's "corner," like the pleasure dome, is a fragile structure built on a precarious foundation. When Jadwin's edifice gives way, it ushers in the return of chaos, the momentary destruction of order and form. Both Kubla Khan and Jadwin, indeed, have a premonition of approaching disaster:

> And 'mid this tumult Kubla heard from far
> Ancestral voices prophesying war! (lines 29–30)

For his part, Jadwin pauses near the door of the Pit just before the final crisis:

> And during the briefest of seconds he could fancy that the familiar bellow

> of its whirling had taken on another pitch. Out of the hideous turmoil, he imagined, there issued a strange unwonted note; as it were, the first rasp and grind of a new avalanche just beginning to stir. (373)

Jadwin's foreboding is soon fulfilled:

> The Pit was mad, was drunk and frenzied; not a man of all those who fought and scrambled and shouted who knew what he or his neighbor did. *They only knew that a support long thought to be secure was giving way,* not gradually . . . but by horrible collapses and equally horrible upward leaps. Now it held, now it broke, now it reformed again, rose again, then again in hideous cataclysms fell from beneath their feet to lower depths than before. . . .
>
> And all the while above the din upon the floor . . . there seemed to thrill and swell that appalling roar of the Wheat itself coming in, coming on like a tidal wave, bursting through, dashing barriers aside, rolling like a measureless, almighty river. (388, my emphasis)

Jadwin's shaping power cannot hold sway indefinitely. Chaos and flux, by nature dynamic and powerful, cannot be contained or transcended by a static structure. Neither Jadwin's "corner" nor his palatial home, complete with his art gallery "shaped like a rotunda, and topped with a vast airy dome of colored glass!" can provide security against subterranean forces—whether in the form of rivers, volcanoes, or earthquakes.

It is the wheat that overturns the order that Jadwin temporarily imposes on the Pit. However, other "subterranean forces" threaten the domestic harmony and aesthetic order capped by Jadwin's airy glass dome. It is *inner* turmoil that threatens the sense of stability achieved by Jadwin after his marriage to Laura. In fact, Jadwin's activity within the Pit, his effort to stay the flood "by the might of his single arm," provides an apt metaphor for his internal struggle: the struggle to keep his own sense of impotence, terror, and chaos at bay. Jadwin's activity within the Pit becomes a desperate fight with the primeval power of the Wheat. Yet Jadwin would seem to prefer desperate struggle with the outer world to the condition of inner emptiness he comes to fear as the alternative.

The nature of Jadwin's fear is clearly articulated in the course of his first exchange with Laura on the subject of his speculation. In Chapter VII Laura extracts from Jadwin a promise to "get out of the market" (231) at the next opportunity. Though Jadwin accedes to Laura's wish, he goes on to express the difficulty he anticipates as a result.

> [Y]ou don't know, you haven't a guess how this trading in wheat gets a hold of you. And, then, what am I to do? What are we fellows, who have made our money to do? I've got to be busy. I can't sit down and twiddle my thumbs. (232)

Jadwin's reference to twiddling his thumbs ominously recalls other characters in Norris's work whose hands lay "idly in [their] lap[s]," after a loss of "occupation" and who turn to obsessive activity in order to fill an inner vacuum.[8]

In the period during which Jadwin, as promised, temporarily abstains from speculative ventures, he is unable to find any other activity with which to fill the void created by his lack of habitual activity. Without a powerful opponent against whom to assert himself, Jadwin feels oppressed by a sense of emptiness that ultimately sends him back into the Pit. It eventually becomes clear, however, that Jadwin's financial activity, even when successful, provides no adequate antidote to his sense of desolation. "'It takes it out of you,'" Jadwin tells Corthell after a great financial coup, "'. . . to make five hundred thousand in about ten hours'" (254). Thus, even profit-making generates, rather than fills, inner emptiness. Making half a million dollars in one working day just "'takes it out of you.'"[9]

Moreover, as Jadwin's financial power and speculative involvement increase, the inner imperative not to be idle, even for a moment, merely grows stronger. Jadwin develops an unspecific physical ailment that causes a muscle spasm every time he begins to fall asleep (321).[10] As long as he is active he manages to "forget these strange symptoms . . . [but] the instant the strain was relaxed, the gallop of hoofs, or as the beat of ungovernable torrents began in his brain" (348; compare 322, 283, 350). Confronted with the unbearable challenge of just "being," passive and relaxed, Jadwin is beset by terror. As long as he is engaged in the effort to impose his will on the external world, he gains a feeling of inner stability. As soon as he relaxes his guard, however, even for an "instant," he is, like Vandover, almost overwhelmed by "ungovernable torrents" welling up from within.

In this sense the Wheat Pit may be viewed as an analogue to Jadwin's inner world. Jadwin's precarious "corner," like his internal equilibrium, is maintained only as a result of the utmost vigilance. Jadwin's inner balance, like Kubla Khan's pleasure dome or like the price of wheat, is constantly in danger of subversion.

The inner dynamic of the Wheat Pit, especially when subjected to Jadwin's manipulation, provides an image for the dialectic of Laura's inner struggle as well. The grounds of this connection emerge clearly from a comparison of two statements made in Chapter X: Page's comment about Laura's emotional state, and Gretry's earlier description of conditions in the Wheat Pit. "'Oh Laura,'" Page cries, in response to a question of Landry's,

> "I don't know her any more these days, she is just like stone—just as though she were crowding down every emotion or any feeling she ever had. She seems to be holding herself in with all her strength . . . and *afraid to let go a finger, for fear she would give way altogether*." (378, my emphasis)

Earlier in the chapter, Gretry expresses his sense of the need to support the price of wheat at its high level. "'[Y]ou saw how freely they sold to us in The Pit yesterday,'" Gretry anxiously tells Jadwin.

> "We've got to buy, and buy and buy, to keep our price up; and look here . . . everything points to a banner crop . . . . The best we can do is to take all the Bears are offering, and support the market. The moment they offer us wheat and we don't buy it, that moment—as you know, yourself,— *they'll throw wheat at you by the train load, and the price will break,* and we with it." (368, my emphasis)

At this juncture, Laura's inner world (like the Wheat Pit itself) cannot be granted even a modicum of free play without being in danger of total collapse. Thus, the Wheat Pit, often reacting violently against human efforts to control prices or responding to natural and political disasters, provides a model for the inner dialectic of the self under pressure, at least as exemplified by Laura and Jadwin.

In the context of these issues, the role of Corthell may be clarified. There is more to the polarity between Jadwin and Corthell than a contrast between Jadwin, the businessman-warrior, and Corthell the aesthete. Certainly Corthell, as Don Graham has brilliantly shown, represents an exclusive aesthetic that shuns Jadwin's sphere of high finance—his world of material success, action, and risk. But as Jadwin's financial maneuvers are part of his struggle both with his most subjective terrors and with his sense of "creation itself," so Corthell's "exclusive aesthetic" serves a number of functions. The portrait of Corthell, like those of Jadwin and Laura, depicts a particularly radical response to the inescapable pressures of existence within a discrete self, surrounded by others, and subject to time. Unlike Jadwin, Corthell has removed himself as far as possible not only from "business" or bad taste in art, decor, and conversation but also from every kind of flux. His chosen aesthetic medium, his clothes, his speech, his studio—all serve to stabilize internal flux, while keeping external signs of mutability to a minimum.

Furthermore, it is not only through aesthetic purity that Corthell seeks stability. He has, in addition, "ordered [his] whole life" (135) around an obsessive love; he has done so almost as thoroughly as Vanamee in *The Octopus*. Corthell's unattainable love is not dead, of course, which saves him from appearing flagrantly grotesque. But the fact that Laura is alive becomes almost insignificant in the context of a character whose inner self and external surroundings are so obsessively changeless as to put him nearly in a class with Vanamee, Maria Macapa, or the sea captain in *Blix*.

When Laura unexpectedly runs into Corthell four years after her marriage, the artist is described as follows:

> It was the old Corthell beyond doubting or denial. Not a single inflection of his low-pitched, gently modulated voice was wanting; not a single infinitesimal mannerism was changed, even to the little tilting of the chin when he spoke, or the quick winking of the eyelids, or the smile that narrowed the corners of the eyes themselves, or the trick of perfect repose of his whole body. Even his handkerchief, as always, since first she had known him, was tucked into his sleeve at the wrist. (239; compare the description of Corthell's studio, 286)

Paralysis such as Corthell's—such thoroughgoing resistance to time, change, and the paradoxes of life—emerges ever more clearly as the greatest "hell" in Norris's fiction. Corthell has made of himself and his surroundings an artificial sanctuary that, like Jadwin's "corner," denies the inevitability of process, change, and multiplicity.

For Laura, however, Corthell's way is intermittently an irresistible temptation. His unchangeability seems the perfect antidote to her own unpredictability, her sense of capriciousness, of being "two Lauras," of not knowing herself—all of which afflict her most acutely just before her marriage and then again once Jadwin's absorption in the Pit keeps him more and more frequently away from home (compare 291). Both the approach of a commitment to intimacy and the loss of such intimacy elicit Laura's inner chaos, which is expressed in spurts of frenetic activity: swift, radical changes of plan, of attire, of emotional commitment.

Corthell's obsessive devotion to Laura climaxes when he remembers her birthday. ("'Remembered!'" he says in response to her surprise; "'I have never forgotten'" [408].) It is, of course, the birthday that Jadwin forgets, and that Laura has staked everything on his remembering. Corthell's unswerving fidelity to Laura offers a refuge, *reductio ad absurdum,* in just the mode that Laura craves. "Everything in life, even death itself, must stand aside while her love [for Jadwin] was put to the test," Laura reflects on the afternoon of her birthday. "Life and death were little things," she muses (in language suggestive of Vanamee); "[l]ove only existed" (401). Laura's birthday plan is for Jadwin to "forget everything else in his love for her" (402). Though Jadwin cannot meet these terms, Corthell is perfectly ready to do so. Like Mephisto trying to make Faust forget Marguerite in the last act of Gounod's opera, Corthell is quite prepared to make Laura "[f]orget everything, everything, everything but that we love each other" (409). Naturally enough, such a proposal has an irresistible appeal for Laura, especially at the very moment that she feels literally forgotten by Jadwin's failure to remember the promise she adjured him to keep "if you love me."

However, Laura's momentary acceptance of Corthell's proposal is rendered in such a way as to suggest that for Laura to accept Corthell's offer is to court the hell that is madness.

> "Don't let me think, then," she cried. "Don't let me think. Make me forget everything, every little hour, every little moment that has passed before this day. Oh, if I remembered once, I would kill you, kill you with my hands! I don't know what I am saying," she moaned, "I don't know what I am

> saying I am mad, I think. . . . What have I said, what have I done, what are you here for?"
>
> "To take you away," he answered gently. . . . "To give my whole life to making you forget that you were ever unhappy."
>
> "And you will never leave me alone—never once?"
>
> "Never, never once."
>
> She drew back from him, looking about the room with unseeing eyes, her fingers plucking and tearing at the lace of her dress; her voice was faint and small, like the voice of a little child.
>
> "I—I am afraid to be alone. Oh, I must never be alone again so long as I shall live. I think I should die." (409–10)

To achieve the vision rendered here is not only to be mad—Ophelia is suggested—but to be entirely paralyzed, without past or future. It is to embrace the possibility of existence within a frozen moment of time, as Mephisto tries persuading Faust to do, knowing that in the very moment of Faust's assent he would belong to the devil.

The sound of wheels under the carriage porch makes Corthell aware of Jadwin's return. "'My husband?'" says Laura:

> "I don't know. She looked up at [Corthell] . . . with unseeing eyes. "Where is my husband? . . . *You are letting me remember*," she cried, in terror. "You are letting me remember. Ah, no no, you don't love me! I hate you." (410–11)

With Jadwin's appearance, Laura cannot help but remember him and, remembering, return to flawed, stubborn, contradictory reality, to pick up the pieces and see what, if anything, is to be done with them. Clearly the question of what Laura in particular, or Laura and Jadwin together, can do with them lies at the imaginative center of the text.

The central problem for Laura, as for Jadwin, is that of *The Pit* as a whole: how to integrate or realize a self and a relationship that will be proof against internal and external chaos. Throughout Norris's work, characters analogous to Corthell provide images of the self defensively buttressed and temporarily secured from danger. Through his obsession with Laura and his rigidly impeccable aesthetic, Corthell effectively stultifies self and experience. If Laura ultimately escapes this option, she does so only by the skin of her teeth.

Art is just one of the methods through which characters in Norris's works commonly try to order or stabilize experience. Repetitive and obsessive behavior is the other typical defense against internal and external stress. For Maria Macapa, Dyke, Vanamee, and others, experience is reduced to a preoccupation with a lost object or the occasion that resulted in loss.

Throughout much of *The Pit,* Laura is certainly preoccupied with Jadwin's absence, but another image of loss recurs with significant regularity and interesting implications. Laura repeatedly returns to her sense of having lost a piece of herself, the self she once was, a loss that crystallizes within Laura's imagination as her memory of the little girl she used to be. Laura often returns to the question of where that little girl has gone; she asks the question of herself, of Jadwin, of Corthell. This recurring motif raises the central question of how the self is to move through time and experience and yet retain unity, without becoming totally stultified in the manner of Corthell and his many precursors in Norris's work.

Laura's first confrontation with her particular sense of loss comes, not surprisingly, on her wedding day. In a scene that recalls *McTeague*'s Trina, envisioning her own prospective loss of self, Laura returns to her old, empty room before driving off with Jadwin after their marriage. Unlike Trina, however, Laura does not capitulate to her fear in one plunge. And although Trina confronts her fear alone while McTeague sleeps soundly in his dental chair, Laura feels Jadwin's hand on her shoulder at the moment of her keenest pain. Jadwin has intuited her feelings, much as Miss Baker ultimately apprehends the desolation that Old Grannis feels in the wake of his own "loss."

The scene between Laura and Jadwin is worth citing in detail. Directly after the wedding ceremony, while the suitcases are being loaded into the carriage in front of the Dearborns' home, Laura runs up the stairs into the house on the pretext of having forgotten something (as indeed she has!). She looks into various rooms, then stops at the door of her own:

> For a long time Laura stood looking silently at the empty room. Here she had lived the happiest period of her life; not an object there, however small, that was not hallowed by association. Now she was leaving it forever. Now the new life, the Untried, was to begin. Forever the old days, the old life

> were gone. Girlhood was gone; the Laura Dearborn that only last night had pressed the pillows of that bed, where was she now? Where was the little black-haired girl of Barrington?
>
> . . . The tears—at last—were in her eyes and the sob in her throat, and she found herself . . . whispering:
>
> "Good-by. Good-by. Good-by."
>
> Then suddenly Laura . . . crossed the room and knelt down at the side of the bed. Her head in her folded arms she prayed—prayed in the unstudied words of her childhood . . . .
>
> And then as she knelt there, all at once she felt an arm, strong, heavy even, laid upon her. She raised her head and looked—for the first time—direct into her husband's eyes.
>
> "I knew—" began Jadwin. "I thought—Dear, I understand, I understand."
>
> He said no more than that. But suddenly Laura knew that he, Jadwin, her husband, did "understand." (186–87)

Laura's confrontation with her fear of losing herself leads to the emotional or spiritual consummation of her marriage to Jadwin. Again, unlike Trina who turns to the certainties and delimiting constraints of a single-minded obsession after confronting her sense of loss, Laura makes contact with Jadwin, looking "—for the first time—direct into her husband's eyes." This is "direct" contact on a new basis, one that includes both recognition of separation from the past and recognition of the pain of separation. As such it appears to provide a viable ground for moving forward, not by denying loss but by reintegrating the emotions stirred by the experience, comforted by the possibilities of human contact.[11]

In Norris's world of internal and external flux, the only ground that emerges for emotional contact, or inner equilibrium, is an acceptance of mutability, flux, and paradox as inevitable aspects of life. In the above scene, at the end of Chapter V (the very center of the text), Laura's girlhood memories promise to become a springboard to the future, rather than a millstone around her neck. The promise is made possible by Jadwin's intuition of Laura's painful sense of loss and by the welling up of love that Laura feels as a result. To relinquish old images of self, but without denying or even forgetting them, would seem to create a possibility for achieving some inner resilience. The implication is that perhaps old images of being may be integrated into a unified self if they can be at once relinquished and sustained. Thus, as in Presley's final words to Hilma in *The Octopus,* recognition and acceptance of loss become a possible basis for life. Indeed, existence becomes tolerable only through recognition and acceptance of its inevitable flux and the incorrigible interrelatedness of pain and joy, gain and loss.

At the end of Chapter V, Laura seems to have found grounds for integrating the loss of the "little black-haired girl" she used to be. However, she quickly takes this tenuous potential as a guarantee of timeless bliss, believing that she now knew

> just what it meant to be completely, thoroughly understood— understood without chance of misapprehension, without shadow of doubt; understood to her heart's heart. . . . How could she be unhappy henceforward? (187)

The very notion of being "completely, thoroughly understood" is comically undercut early in the novel when, in response to a haphazard remark of Laura's, Landry Court passionately cries, "'Ah . . . you don't know what it *means* to me to look into the eyes of a woman who really understands.'" This exclamation bewilders Laura, who stares at him "wondering just what she had said" (140). (Landry later repeats this line to Page, who has the good sense openly to wonder what he means by it.) Provisional contact or understanding is difficult enough to achieve; absolute, unambiguous, unchanging certainty in human relations, as in the Wheat Pit or within the self, is inherently impossible. Laura's need for unequivocal permanence in love is precisely what makes her susceptible to Corthell.

The scene between Laura and Jadwin at the end of Chapter V may be taken as the beginning, but also the high point, of loving contact between them. Its implications are extended by the final event of the chapter—Laura's unwitting fulfillment of her promise to kiss Jadwin "spontaneously" one day. Earlier in the chapter, Jadwin had noted that in the course of their engagement Laura had never kissed him "'of [her] own accord'" (177), and he had proposed to make a "bargain" with her. "'We'll call it a bargain,'" he had said.

> "Some day—before very long, mind you—you are going to kiss me—that

> way, understand, of your own accord, when I'm not thinking of it; and I'll get that conservatory [built the way you wanted]. . . . Is it a bargain? . . . What do you say?" (176–77)

Laura agrees, though a contractual agreement for a spontaneous kiss is clearly a contradiction in terms. Indeed, the scene in which the agreement is fulfilled suggests that the fulfillment is meaningful only insofar as the "bargain" itself has been forgotten.

"'You were wrong,'" Laura tells Jadwin after kissing him at the end of Chapter V.

> "[R]emember that time in the library when you said I was undemonstrative. I'm not. I love you dearly, dearly, and never for once, for one little moment am I ever going to allow you to forget it."
>
> Suddenly, . . . an idea occurred to [Jadwin].
>
> "Oh, our bargain—remember? You didn't forget, after all."
>
> "I did. I did," she cried. "I did forget it. That's the very sweetest thing about it." (187–88)

This scene, which renders the fulfillment of the promise to remember by forgetting, dramatizes one of the paradoxes at the heart of the novel. The very attempt to insure an emotional response through a "bargain" or "promise" is inevitably doomed. In addition, although Laura has benignly forgotten the agreement when she comes to fulfill it, her kiss is followed ominously by her feeling that "never for once, for one little moment am I ever going to allow you to forget, [that I love you]" (187–88). The need never to forget, or never "to allow [Jadwin] to forget," turns memory into a coercive weapon, a weapon that inevitably fails to work. Laura's wish never to forget her love easily translates into her subsequent intention of forcing Jadwin to forget everything except his love for her. Her demand that Corthell make her forget her own life ("'every little hour, every little moment that has passed before this day'") is only one more step in the same direction.

At the beginning of the novel, Laura is powerfully attracted by two contradictory versions of the world as rendered in Genesis. One of these may be identified with Corthell, the other with Jadwin. Utterly enchanted by the opera in Chapter I, Laura sits "spellbound, her hands clasped tight, her every faculty of attention at its highest pitch" (20). It is in this context that Laura imagines herself dying "beautifully, gently, in some garden far away—[dying] . . . amid the flowers and the birds, in some far-off place where it was always early morning and where there was soft music" (21). This is an image of Paradise in Corthell's style, a sentimental, romantic image reminiscent once again (like Vanamee's "idyl" or the old diver's memory in *Blix*) of Keats's urn or the speaker's flight with the nightingale, to an exquisite realm of utter stasis.[12]

We have already seen, however, that another side of Laura is as fascinated by the giant city outside the opera as by the world projected on the stage. Ultimately, Laura identifies her vision of the city's "infinite, inexhaustible vitality" (62) with "the thing that isn't meant to be seen, as though it were too elemental, too—primordial; like the first verses of Genesis" (63).[13] This notion, furthermore, leads to the idea of "men for whom all this crash of conflict and commerce had no terrors" (63). Obviously Jadwin is for Laura such a man, and in choosing him over Corthell, Laura acts on an impulse to contend with flux, even though she does not ultimately succeed in fulfilling the potential implicit in her choice.

Laura and Jadwin's exchange in the "Conclusion" of the novel confirms not only the positive potential of embracing flux and paradox but also Laura's own difficulty doing so. At the end of *The Pit,* Laura and Jadwin are leaving Chicago, stripped of their wealth, heading West to start over again. As they sit on their suitcases waiting to be taken to the train, Laura reads Jadwin a letter she herself has not finished reading—a letter from her newly married sister Page. In a postscript to the letter, Page mentions having run into Sheldon Corthell in New York.

> "Oh," said Jadwin, as Laura put the letter quickly down, "Corthell—that artist chap. By the way, whatever became of him?"
>
> Laura settled a comb in the back of her hair.
>
> "He went away," she said. "You remember—I told you— told you all about it."
>
> She would have turned away her head, but he laid a hand upon her shoulder.
>
> "I remember" he answered, looking squarely into her eyes, "I remember nothing—only that I have been to blame for everything. I told you once—

> long ago—that I *understood.* And I understand now . . . as I never did before." (417)

This scene unmistakably recalls the end of Chapter V. Jadwin's hand on Laura's shoulder, and his direct look into her eyes, culminate in his reference to the conversation on their wedding day. However, what Jadwin "understands" has now changed. And Jadwin's "'I remember nothing'" suggests more clearly than before his own readiness to affirm one of the text's basic paradoxes: the possibility of remembering and forgetting at one and the same time.

Jadwin's return home after his financial ruin—on Laura's birthday—is, in a sense, a replay of the paradoxical drama in which Laura, by kissing Jadwin, unintentionally fulfills her promise to him without realizing it. The action of *The Pit* is indeed "framed" not only by the dramas in the Pit and in the opera *Faust,* but also by the two emotional contracts agreed on by Laura and Jadwin: the "bargain" for a kiss, initiated by Jadwin during his engagement to Laura, and the birthday promise, elicited by Laura in a misguided effort to salvage their marriage.[14]

While Laura's spontaneous kiss in Chapter V is the more genuine fulfillment of her promise insofar as that promise has been forgotten, Jadwin's unwitting return home in Chapter X, according to his own forgotten agreement, is not a fulfillment in this sense. Both he and Laura have come too close to being shattered by the ties they have nearly destroyed for their relationship to be so easily revitalized. Perhaps the seed for renewal is contained in Jadwin's presumably deliberate "I remember . . . nothing," especially since his words imply grounds for containing complexity. Yet Jadwin's own sense of "starting in all over again" (417) appears problematic. The novel has presented too many "new" starts that have not sustained themselves (compare 142, 186).

Even more ominous, however, is Laura's refusal to bestow even a parting glance on the house she is leaving behind. Before the carriage begins to move, Jadwin rubs the fog from the window:

> "Well," said Jadwin . . . "look your last at the old place, Laura. You'll never see it again."

> But she would not look.
> "No, no," she said. "I'll look at you, dearest, at you and our future, which is to be happier than any years we have ever known.'" (418–19)

The final image in the novel underscores the problematic nature of Laura's refusal, at this juncture, to look back. Almost immediately after Laura states her intention of looking exclusively at the "happy" future, something familiar presses upon her consciousness:

> [S]he was aware of a certain familiarity in the neighborhood the carriage was traversing. The strange sense of having lived through this scene, these circumstances, once before, took hold upon her. (420)

Laura cannot at first identify the vaguely familiar scene. Then, "[a]ll at once, intuitively, Laura turned in her place and raising the flap that covered the little window at the back of the carriage, looked behind" (420) to recognize the Board of Trade, home of the Pit. Thus, the final image of the novel—like the closing image of the first chapter—is Laura's vision of the Pit. Described in language that clearly echoes the closing lines of Chapter I, the Board of Trade appears

> black, monolithic, crouching on its foundations like a monstrous sphinx with blind eyes, silent, grave—crouching there without a sound, without a sign of life, under the night and the drifting veil of rain. (421)

This image suggests a creature, silent and immobile, as if not there, yet "crouching in the dark" implicitly waiting to spring, regardless of whether Laura agrees to look back or not. The sphinx image, with its connotations of *Oedipus Rex*—perhaps the greatest Western tragedy of mystery, self-knowledge, and the inextricable interrelations between forgetting and remembering, the past and the present, life and death—provides no reassurance as to the future of Laura and Curtis Jadwin. In this context, the notion of the Oedipus legend as a paradigm for narrative itself adds a provocative grace note to my argument.[15]

The novel ends with Laura and Jadwin restored to one another, hopeful and intent on starting over, a world of new possibilities before them. But while the novel seems to end with a forward thrust, Laura and Jadwin seem, in a sense, to be returning to the past rather than preparing for new challenges.

Despite the hopeful moment at the end of Chapter V, Laura never finds a sustaining connection between her past and present selves. Her sense of disjunction and loss recurs, like her memory of the little girl picking blackberries in Barrington. The narrative voice speaks of the change in Laura after her first three years of marriage as "so swift . . . that it was not so much a growth as a transformation. . . . She looked back upon the Miss Dearborn of [the State Street . . .] days as though she were another person" (203).

Jadwin, moreover, has his own memories, analogous to Laura's "lost" little black-haired girl. "'It struck me as kind of queer, the way things have turned out for me, . . .'" Jadwin tells Gretry in the art gallery of his palatial house.

> Sam, do you know, I remember the time, up there in Ottawa County, Michigan, on my old dad's farm, when I used to have to get up before daybreak to tend the stock, and my sister and I used to . . . stand in the warm cow fodder . . . to warm our bare feet. (200)

Like Laura, Jadwin is stymied by the sense of disjuncture between "then" and "now"; however, his emphasis on the queerness of "the way things have turned out" perhaps implies a demand for some connection between past and present, rather than mere grief at the irretrievability of the past, such as Laura repeatedly expresses.

This passage culminates in Jadwin's recollection of his younger sister's death and his wish to rewrite history. Having removed himself from the harsh existence he shared with her, Jadwin feels that he would "'like to have made it up to her'" (200). This is a fleeting wish on Jadwin's part; he is not, after all, Vanamee. Yet Jadwin's impulse helps explain, among other things, the private drama he enacts with Hargus, the ruined speculator who has loitered near the Pit for years in a greasy coat, reading old newspapers. One of the rare moments of satisfaction Jadwin achieves as a result of his "corner" comes when he forces the man who sold Hargus out twenty years earlier to write Hargus a check for nearly half a million dollars. Subsequently Hargus, the check still in his hand, pleads with Jadwin to give him a stock-market "tip." "'Just a little tip. My God, I could make fifty dollars by noon'" (344). This scene dramatizes the impossibility of effecting a direct revision of the past, as Jadwin attempts. Such a reading of the scene is reinforced by the fact that Hargus appears to have lost the whole fortune Jadwin restores to him, even before Jadwin's own corner breaks (372).

Jadwin's intermittent doubts about the value of his wealth are related both to the problem of the self in stasis and to the problem of integrating the past rather than seeking a way to relive it. Laura tells Corthell how she looks "'back with regret and with longing toward a joyous and simple childhood'" (294), as Jadwin talks to Laura about his own boyhood and his sense that he was

> "happy then. Of course I've got you now, and that's all the difference in the world. . . . But I don't know. . . . If they'd let me be and put us two—just you and me—back in the old house with the bare floors and the rawhide chairs and the shuck beds, I guess we'd manage . . . sometimes I think that we'd be happier—you and I—just chumming along, shoulder to shoulder, poor an' working hard, than making big money an' spending big money." (313)

Laura and Jadwin are, to a certain extent, restored to just such a (rather sentimental) possibility at the end of the novel. Thus, what seems like a resolution, a salvation, may also be seen as another kind of escape. Jadwin and Laura, at the end of *The Pit,* are like children who cling to one another hand in hand as they walk out of the garden. (Laura even cites *Paradise Lost* in the last pages of the text.) They have, indeed, all but literally returned to the individual childhoods for which they longed—at least to a time before Jadwin made "big money," the time of his and Laura's sweetest memories.

The clock, however, cannot be turned back, as Jadwin's maneuver with Hargus most clearly implies. Page, furthermore, reports Landry's conviction that Jadwin will surely make another vast fortune or two out West. It is as good a prediction as any. Certainly the models of reformed speculators provided by the text (Hargus, Cressler, Jadwin himself at the start of the novel) offer no ground for believing that Jadwin's "cure" is permanent.

The issues raised by Laura and Jadwin's experience, then, are intricate and remain unresolved at the end of the novel, despite passing intimations of potential grounds for resolution. One crucial component of any resolution would seem to be a constructive role for memory within the economy of the self, such as Jadwin's final attitude implies. Perhaps the one other model for value or self-integration provided by *The Pit* is to be found in the figure of Laura's sister Page. Don Graham considers the Page-Landry plot of *The Pit* Norris's masterpiece, and as a parody of Laura's love-life, histrionics, and aesthetic opinions, it is often both sharp and hilarious.

At another level, however, Page's experience suggests, in a lighter vein, a resolution of many issues raised by the story of Laura and Jadwin. Page Dearborn, with her earnestness, her moral fervor, her impeccably neat writing desk and her voluminous journal provides an image of experience that serves as more than a comic contrast to Laura.[16] In some way Page (both alone and in her relationship with Landry) embodies a state of being that, will-she-nill-she, is a hybrid of mixed modes almost as random as life itself—and precisely for that reason perhaps flexible enough to thrive.

The scene before Laura's wedding presents a typical view of Page. She and Aunt Wess sit in the empty church before the ceremony with their tension and anxiety rising. Aunt Wess calms herself in her own habitual way by counting the pews, while Page repeats the litany. Page's efforts at self-control break down, however, once Laura appears. "'There's the last of Laura,' she whimpered. 'There's the last of my dear sister for me . . . she'll never be the same to me after now,' sobbed Page" (182–83). Unfortunately, Miss Gretry, who seems always to do the wrong thing at the wrong time, gets the hiccups at this juncture so that "Page could not restrain a giggle, and the giggle strangled with the sobs in her throat so that the little girl was not far from hysterics" (183). Page pulls herself together just in time, with the help of the ritual order created by the familiar words filling the church at that moment: "'Dearly beloved we are gathered together here in the sight of God'" (183).

In this scene, as in others, Page runs the gamut of incongruous feelings that render her comic, but far from despicable. At Laura's wedding, Page mixes giggles and hiccups with sobs, just as she often loves and hates Laura with equal intensity. Though she weeps for the loss of Laura, she nonetheless follows Laura from the past into the future, full of contradictory feelings toward her, but always ready to assume responsibility for her emotions as well as her views.

Even Page's literary pretensions are no more than she can integrate into her relationships with others. Her library scene with Landry Court is a comic combination of emotional intensities and misguided "intellectual" discourse; yet Page and Landry, for their naive emotional honesty alone, are quite irresistible. In Chapter VI, with Jadwin's passion for speculation sharply on the rise, we find that Page has "lectured [Landry] solemnly on the fact that he was over-absorbed in business and was starving his soul" (218). Page's remedy, as her name might suggest, is a "course of reading" for Landry, who declares himself ready and willing for treatment. Thus, the couple retires to the Jadwin library one evening. Page speaks of Ruskin and Lamb; Landry of "the 'newest book.'"

> But Page never read new books; she was not interested, and their talk, unable to establish itself upon a common ground, halted, and was in a fair way to end, until at last, and by insensible degrees, they began to speak of themselves and of each other. Promptly they were all aroused. (218)

In the conversation that follows, Page and Landry (Norris's latter-day Paolo and Francesca?) express many feelings and ideas, some of which, both in themselves and in combination are very funny. "'You are beautifully womanly,'" Landry tells Page just before he leaves,

> ". . . and so high-minded and well read. It's been inspiring to me, I want you should know that. Yes, sir, a real inspiration. It's been inspiring, elevating, to say the least."
>
> "I like to read, if that's what you mean," she hastened to say.
>
> "By Jove, I've got to do some reading too. . . . I'll make time. I'll get that "Stones of Venice" I've heard you speak of, and I'll sit up nights—and keep awake with black coffee—but I'll read that book from cover to cover." (222)

Page and Landry's efforts at a "cultural evening" may be sharply contrasted with the finesse and "good taste" of Corthell's carefully manipulated visit with Laura in the art gallery. Corthell's flawless rendering of Mendelssohn's "Consolation," Beethoven's "Appassionata," and finally Liszt's "Mephisto Walzer," are a fitting beginning for his would-be seduction of Laura.[17] "'Oh,'" Laura comments as Corthell's last organ notes fade into silence, "'that was wonderful, wonderful. It is like a new language—no, it is like new thoughts, too fine for language'" (252).

Corthell's subtle and harmonious blend of aesthetic and erotic modes creates an expressive context that may not be "too fine for language," but that reveals a function of art unexplored by Jadwin, Page and Landry.[18] Compared with Corthell's aesthetic and sentimental "education" of Laura, Page's effort to edify Landry appears naive and comic. Its moral content is unmistakably superior, however, and moral content is by no means irrelevant. In Corthell's hands, Mendelssohn's "Consolation" and Beethoven's "Appassionata" provide a camouflage for consolation and passion of a very different kind. Of course Page and Landry "use" art almost as purposively as Corthell. But they are unaware of their own motives, and their blindness is not merely a source of comedy. When juxtaposed with Corthell's premeditation, Page's and Landry's lack of self-consciousness becomes a measure of their value.

If Page is comic, she is also full of vitality, as well as a range of strong feelings that do not frighten her. It is Page who sees clearly what is happening to Laura, who risks confronting Laura at more than one crucial emotional juncture, but who also understands the limits of her possible effectiveness when she seeks to intervene in Laura's life. Even Page's relation to the past appears more vital, as well as more viable, than Laura's. At the end of the novel, in her New York letter to Laura, Page can speak of the "palace on North Avenue" adding, "'Never, never, will I forget that house'" (415). Page can remember the past without being haunted by it on the one hand, or compelled (like Laura) to avoid seeing or thinking of it.

Landry, too, is comic, with his eager-beaver readiness to drink black coffee in order to stay awake through Page's literary lessons. Yet he nonetheless constitutes an image of human vitality as well.[19] Unlike Corthell, Landry passes beyond his "love" for Laura to the relationship with Page (for which he is much better suited), thus exemplifying the possibility of moving through experience without either calcification or disintegration. His love for and loyalty to Jadwin provides further support for the notion of Landry as a small touchstone of value within the novel. It is Landry who clings to Jadwin during his worst hour in the Pit; Landry who, with tears on his face, tries to protect Jadwin, never doubting his mentor's value, while

Laura sits at home counting the minutes and wondering whether Jadwin has forgotten her birthday. Landry and Page, separately and together, seem capable of a wider range of feeling and even expression, either than Corthell, or than Laura and Jadwin themselves.

Thus, *The Pit* would appear to suggest that the only way to live without being paralyzed, or mad (like Jadwin and Laura at various points near the end of the novel), is to accept the possibility of mixed aesthetic modes, like unexpected combinations in life itself, but to do so from a point of inner equilibrium—not like Laura donning one splendid dress after another, or playing Phèdre, Portia, and Athalie in turn. Laura's "acting" is presented as an attempt at emotional consolidation, or self-integration. However, Laura never manages to integrate her capacity to "act" many roles, her insistence on being "anything [she] . . . choose[s]" (310), and her simultaneous need for inviolable stability within which her husband would be "always" the same (314), "as much her own as her very hands" (402). Indeed, at the end of *The Pit,* she hopes that this has been insured, but the text has provided many grounds for doubting the desirability, as well as the possibility, of any such static Paradise.

Within *The Pit* Corthell is the most extreme example of the attempt to achieve certainty by buttressing the self against all flux. Yet even he cannot gain his ends, except in relation to inanimate objects. To be sure, Corthell—unlike Vandover or Presley—has at least chosen his aesthetic medium wisely. He uses his artistic gift for interior decoration and nonmimetic art: Corthell makes stained-glass windows, and miniatures at that. Unlike Presley's poem, or Vandover's effort to grapple with his "Last Enemy" on canvas, Corthell's art certainly has the advantage of avoiding everything that approximates threat. Few other characters in Norris's work are as successful as Corthell in finding a mode through which to contain internal and external turmoil without appearing blatantly grotesque.

Thus the central issue in *The Pit,* as elsewhere in Norris's work, is whether to stultify experience in memory and art, or subject it to flux and tolerate immersion in fluidity (Condy's and Annixter's choice), at once eschewing the Quixotic compulsion to dominate flux and yet avoiding destruction by external or internal chaos.

The Pit provides only a few tentative images of potential resolution—more, however, than in Norris's earlier work. The character and experience of Laura and Jadwin occasionally suggest the possibility of moving through time and space with a full consciousness of the need to accept loss, paradox, and change as inevitable. The character and experience of Page and Landry serve more consistently, though in a subordinate mode, to suggest a possibility of being that includes laughter, tears, giggles, hiccups, absurdity, and bad taste, as well as love, loyalty, emotional flexibility, and a modicum of intellectual and aesthetic pleasure. Indeed, Page and Landry's motley range of reading matter and the very gaucherie and naiveté of Page's mercurial journal emerge as preferable to the coercive purity of Corthell. While Corthell's purity seems to Laura "too fine for language," Page and Landry's acceptance of mixed modes in narrative art, as well as life, becomes the final measure of value within the Norris canon.

Afterword: A Parting Glance

"The moment of aesthetic vision lifts us out of the flux."

—Edwin Muir

In "The Jongleur of Taillebois," one of Norris's earliest stories (1892), a murderer who has successfully hidden his crime for many years is finally exposed when he tries to perform a song with a musical instrument that disobeys his commands. Instead of playing the tune intended by the singer, the "vielle" emits first the notes of the murdered man's favorite song, and then the "precise musical imitation" of the victim's scream of death. Amelot, the singer, dashes the instrument to the ground only to recognize the splintered wood of the Taillebois forest, scene of long-forgotten bloodshed. At the sight, Amelot himself begins to speak, without recognizing his own voice, immediately thereafter "endeavoring, yet fearing, to recollect what he had confessed" (15).

Amelot's instrument, made of wood from a tree that grew over the dead man's burial-place, is perhaps Norris's first symbol of the return of the repressed, the process by which what is apparently forgotten and buried deep within the self involuntarily returns with a vengeance, clamoring for expression. "The Jongleur," with its medieval setting, violent plot, and gruesome details uncannily prefigures the preoccupations that inform even Norris's mature work. Not only does the story begin with death, and denial of death, but the growth of the tree and the wanderings of the murderer evoke both the inevitable passage of time and the gradual, yet multiple, changes wrought thereby. Finally, the climax of the tale involves sudden, unexpected devastation—stock-in-trade of the naturalistic mode. But it also crystallizes the human and aesthetic issues I have been tracing in Norris's work. Amelot's self-betrayal in his own effort to sing and make music becomes an evocative image of the tension between aesthetic form and the experience it would order, express, or efface.

The Pit, completed shortly before Norris's sudden death in 1902, contains a rich transmutation not only of the substance of these issues but also of the narrative mode within which they find their earliest expression. By the time of *The Pit*, memory is no longer primarily a vehicle of sudden destruction, or the medium for compulsive reenactment in Norris's work. As we have seen, it has instead become a force that can facilitate the integration of experience. Progressively, Norris's emphasis has shifted to the unfolding and the mastery of experience within the confines of the discrete individual who struggles for control, at least of his or her own inner life. The possibility of meaningful expression—communication transmitted and received—has come to replace both obsessive storytelling and sudden, involuntary confession of horror; it has begun to resolve the drama of a self divided against itself.

In an essay written in 1901, Norris makes a distinction between the "artful[ness]" of a "well composed, well balanced" book and one that is built on "the artificial stimulation of one exciting episode after another" ("Remaining Seven Weekly Letters," 62). This distinction may reflect some of the changes in Norris's own mode of storytelling during the ten years between "The Jongleur" and *The Pit*. The formal clarity of *The Pit*, its artful structure and lack of blatant contrivance, is perhaps an expression of Norris's own increasingly successful fronting of change at all levels. In his last work of fiction, Norris's often repetitive ideological statements have all but disappeared and have dramatically shifted in function. At the same time, his work exhibits a growing recognition of flux as the inevitable condition of life and progressively affirms the individual's capacity to derive strength from the consciousness of mutability itself.

Norris's own work becomes an increasingly flexible mode of expression, a source of satisfaction for Norris, and perhaps even a sign of inner mastery. His last novel is certainly his most complex and subtle exploration of the function of memory and art. As we have seen, Corthell's stultifying and distancing use of aesthetic form provides a foil to the novel-reading of Page, Landry, and Jadwin. And Page, with her private journal and her budding correspondence, becomes the first "writer" in Norris's work (since Ward Bennett) who ventures to sing directly of herself.

We cannot say where Norris's next work might have led him, but by the time of his death, he had already put the "boy Zola" within him at some distance. In fact, by the time of *The Pit,* Henry James has become a more meaningful analogue than Émile Zola. In his effort to make the character of Laura the central focus of the text, in his structuring of Laura's choices among three suitors, in the polarity of the brash businessman and the dilettantish aesthete, Norris might have been "rewriting" *The Portrait of a Lady.*[1] Had Norris lived, the Jamesian impulse—or other, equally unexpected affiliations for a "naturalist"—might even have led him to tap the experimental possibilities, not of science but of narrative structure. Certainly his general awareness of literary movements and his sustained interest in the functions of memory and aesthetic form might eventually have led him to an interest in Joyce, Woolf, or Proust.

Perhaps, as time went on, he would have made a great deal more of that "capacious gift" that Alfred Kazin suggests "he had not even begun to exhaust when he died" (75). Of course, we cannot predict the direction of a development that did not take place. But if Norris was prevented, like Annixter, from developing his fullest potential, the least we can do is give him full credit for his realized achievements.

Notes

Notes to Chapter 1: Norris's Dubious Naturalism

1. On the initial popularity of Norris's work, see Don Graham, Introduction to *Critical Essays on Frank Norris,* xv-xii; James D. Hart, *The Popular Book,* 220; Joseph R. McElrath, Jr., Introduction to *Frank Norris: The Critical Reception,* ix-xxiv, *passim.*

2. Norris began work on both *Vandover and the Brute* and *McTeague* while at Harvard in 1894–1895. *McTeague* was published in 1899, while *Vandover* appeared only posthumously, in 1914. Thus, *Moran of the Lady Letty,* published serially in 1898, appeared before either *Vandover* or *McTeague.* I begin with the latter, however, because Norris lavished sustained effort on them before beginning *Moran* and because *Vandover* and *McTeague* may be considered major, while *Moran* may not. Donald Pizer's formulation that "*Moran* is absurd, *Blix* slight, and *A Man's Woman* tedious" (*The Novels of Frank Norris,* 86) has summarized the general critical consensus on Norris's "popular novels" for nearly twenty years. Despite a few recent suggestions that Norris took more care with *Blix* than has been apparent (Debra D. Munn, "The Revision of Frank Norris's *Blix,*" 47–55) and had more ironic intentions in *Moran* than have been perceived (Joseph R. McElrath, Jr., "The Erratic Design of Frank Norris's *Moran of the Lady Letty,*" 114–24), these texts remain most interesting insofar as they illuminate strains within Norris's major fiction.

3. Before turning seriously to literature, the young Norris spent two years studying art in Paris, where Zola's work was drawing the attention of both the critics and the public. Whether or not Norris actually read Zola's fiction during this period (1887–1889), he could not have avoided contact with the controversy over realism that was raging at the time. Both *McTeague* and *Vandover* clearly show that by 1899 Norris knew at least *L'Assommoir, La Bête humaine,* and *Thérèse Raquin* backward and forward. Lars Åhnebrink and Marius Biencourt have provided ample evidence of Zola's influence on Norris's later work as well. See Lars Åhnebrink, *The Beginnings of Naturalism in American Fiction,* especially sections V:3, VI:5, and X:3; and Marius Biencourt, *Une influence du naturalisme français en Amérique: Frank Norris,* 81–84, 93–95, 99–100, 116–231 *passim.*

4. Jesse S. Crisler and Joseph R. McElrath, Jr., *Frank Norris: A Reference Guide,* xii.

5. Donald Pizer, "The Problem of Philosophy in the Novel," 54–57; compare Don Graham, *The Fiction of Frank Norris: The Aesthetic Context,* 1–2; Joseph R. McElrath, Jr., "Frank Norris's *Vandover and the Brute,*" 29; Charles Child Walcutt, *American Literary Naturalism: A Divided Stream,* 122–23.

6. Graham, *Fiction of Frank Norris,* 2.

7. See Chapter 3.

8. See Charles L. Crow, "The Real Vanamee and His Influence on Frank Norris's *The Octopus*," 137–38; Richard Allen Davison, "Frank Norris's *The Octopus*," 107–8; William B. Dillingham, "Frank Norris and the Genteel Tradition," 61, 64–65; James K. Folsom, "Social Darwinism or Social Protest? The 'Philosophy' of *The Octopus*," 393–94; Graham, *Fiction of Frank Norris*, 119–22; George W. Johnson, *Frank Norris and Romance*, 522–63; Joseph R. McElrath, Jr., "Frank Norris's *The Octopus*," 139; George Wilbur Meyer, "A New Interpretation of *The Octopus*," 359; Pizer, *The Novels of Frank Norris*, 135–40; William Vance, "Romance in *The Octopus*," 132–34; compare Mark Seltzer, "The Naturalist Machine," 118.
9. For an analysis of the Trina plot within *McTeague*, see Chapter 4. For the critical debate over Trina's decline, see Chapter 4, n. 14
10. Graham, *Fiction of Frank Norris*, 1.
11. Compare Walcutt, *American Literary Naturalism*, 115–17; Franklin Walker, *Frank Norris: A Biography*, 58–59, 257.
12. Compare "Frank Norris's Weekly Letter," 73–75; "A Problem in Fiction: Truth vs. Accuracy," 55–58, 203–4.
13. Compare Walcutt, *American Literary Naturalism*, 116.
14. Graham, *Fiction of Frank Norris*, 7.
15. Pizer, *The Novels of Frank Norris*, 15.
16. Compare McElrath, "The Erratic Design of *Moran*," 116.
17. Compare Arnold Goldsmith, "The Development of Frank Norris's Philosophy," 181–83. A likely source for Norris's sketch that has not, to my knowledge, been noted is Rudyard Kipling's "Her Majesty's Servants," which first appeared in 1895.
18. I take the phrase "quest for certitude" from an article by Reuven Tsur.
19. Keats, letter to George and Thomas Keats, 21 December 1817.
20. Compare Chapters 2 and 5.
21. Letter to Benjamin Bailey, 22 November 1817 (274). Compare the letter to James Augustus Hessey, 9 October 1818: "The Genius of Poetry must work out its own salvation in a man: It cannot be matured by law and precept, but by sensation and watchfulness in itself" (328–29). And Frank Norris:

> [T]he art of fiction has no handbook[;] . . . from the study of your fellows you shall learn more than from the study of all the textbooks that ever will be written.
>
> But to do this you must learn to sit very quiet and be very watchful, and so train your eyes and ears that every sound and sight shall be significant to you. ("Novelists of the Future: The Training They Need," 12–13)

22. See Frank Norris, "An Opening for Novelists," 30; Frank Norris, "Storytellers vs. Novelists," 66; Donald Pizer's general Introduction to *Literary Criticism of Frank Norris*, xiii-xxii, and his Introduction to "Life, Not Literature," 19–24; compare *Blix*, 227–28 and 273; and *Moran of the Lady Letty*, 234. For a recent contribution on Norris's understanding of these two terms, see Mary Lawlor, "'Life' and 'Literature' in Frank Norris's Cowboy Tales," 34–40 *passim*.
23. See Chapter 2.

24. Compare Ernst Marchand, *Frank Norris: A Study,* 231; Pizer, *The Novels of Frank Norris,* 17, 21–22.
25. Compare Joseph McElrath's view that Norris comes to see change as possible, but only at the level of the self, or of individual relationships ("Frank Norris's *The Octopus*: The Christian Ethic as Pragmatic Response," 145).
26. See Joseph Katz's view of Jadwin's illness ("Eroticism in American Realism," 48); compare Maxwell Geismar, *Rebels and Ancestors: The American Novel 1890–1915,* 56–57.
27. In "Corporate Fiction," Benn Michaels explores other implications of the elusive S. Behrman (193–95).
28. Compare Warren G. French's emphasis on Norris's transcendentalist affinities (*Frank Norris,* 37–39, 91, 94, 137–38); compare Donald Pizer, "Another Look at *The Octopus*," 219, 224.
29. Compare Charles Norris's account of having read his brother's notebook and been "soundly kicked for [his] impertinence" (8).
30. Graham, *Fiction of Frank Norris,* 13.
31. Compare Lars Åhnebrink on the connection between *A Man's Woman* and Ibsen's *Brand* (*The Beginnings of Naturalism,* 389–99).

Notes to Chapter 2: The Power of the Word

1. See "An Opening for Novelists," 29–30; Letter to Isaac F. Marcosson (*The Letters of Frank Norris,* 30–31). Compare *Blix,* 228.
2. For emphases on Norris's "story-telling" gift, see Charles Norris, *Frank Norris,* 1; Franklin Walker, *Frank Norris: A Biography,* xi, 1–4, 58–59, 257; Burgess cited in Joseph R. McElrath, Jr., "Frank Norris: Early Posthumous Responses," 38; compare Frederic Taber Cooper, *Some American Storytellers,* v-vi.
3. Dedication to *The Pit.* Compare Charles Norris's references to this period in *Frank Norris,* 2.
4. Compare Baruch Hochman, "On the Imagination of Death," 36–37.
5. The end of *The Pit* also contains other echoes from the end of *Blix*: an unopened letter, lost innocence, leaving the Garden, and specific references to remembering and forgetting. See Chapter 6.
6. Compare Don Graham's discussion of McTeague and Trina's aesthetic possessions in *The Fiction of Frank Norris: The Aesthetic Context* (50–53 especially).
7. Joseph R. McElrath, Jr., "Frank Norris's *The Octopus*: The Christian Ethic as Pragmatic Response," 147.
8. Graham, *Fiction of Frank Norris,* 68–71.
9. Compare Benn Michaels, "Corporate Fiction," 212–13.
10. "The Genius of Poetry must work out its own salvation in a man: It cannot be matured by law and precept but by sensation and watchfulness in itself" (Keats to James Augustus Hessey, 9 October 1818). Compare "Novelists of the Future: The Training They Need," 12–13.
11. Compare Richard Allen Davison, "A Reading of Frank Norris's *The Pit*," 84.

12. Joseph R. McElrath, Jr., "Frank Norris: A Biographical Essay," 229, 231.
13. Charles Norris, *Frank Norris,* 14.

Notes to Chapter 3: *Vandover and the Brute:* The Failure of Memory and Art

1. It is this memory, for example, that suddenly invades Vandover's consciousness as he tries to escape a painful memory of more recent origin—that of Ida Wade's suicide, which, from Vandover's point of view, he has caused. Compare Edwin Haviland Miller, "The Art of Frank Norris in *Vandover and the Brute*," 59–60; and Mark Seltzer, "The Naturalist Machine," 140–42. Miller's emphasis is the connection between the death of Vandover's mother and his seduction of Ida. Seltzer's concern is the movement from the "disconnected pictures" of Vandover's memory to the "sequential plotting" of the narrative itself. For Seltzer the steam engine in the death scene of Chapter I is a central image not only within Vandover's disconnected "memory pictures" but also for Norris's "mechanics of fiction," which Seltzer calls a "mechanics of power."
2. The phrase "pliable character" often recurs. See *Vandover and the Brute,* 294, 303, 384, 461, 519, 524. The same idea is also repeated in other terms. Compare 295, 468, 497, 548, 558. Vandover's "fatal adaptability" (558)—like that of Zola's Gervaise—is not only taken for granted by Vandover and the narrative voice; it is often accepted at face value by critics of the novel. See William B. Dillingham, *Frank Norris: Instinct and Art,* 69; Lars Åhnebrink, *The Beginnings of Naturalism in American Fiction,* 291. Critics have also assumed that the narrator (and Norris) fully support Van's sense of his disease as a deserved punishment. See William B. Dillingham, "Frank Norris and the Genteel Tradition," 196–97; Charles Hoffman, "Norris and the Responsibility of the Novelist," 510–11; Robert W. Schneider, "Frank Norris: The Naturalist as Victorian," 16–18. Compare Lee Clark Mitchell, "Little Pictures on the Lacquered Surfaces," 389–90.
3. Compare Miller, "The Art of Frank Norris in *Vandover*," 56–57.
4. The Mazatlan itself is referred to as a "damnt ole tub" (390) by the Jew who later drowns.
5. See *Vandover,* 370, 469, 493. Van sees Haight's fate as "unjustified. . . . Vandover would gladly have changed places with him" (548). Unquestionably, if Haight's fate had been his own, it would have seemed appropriate. "'We're both ruined,'" Vandover says to Haight, "'only in your case it wasn't your fault'" (548).
6. Compare Don Graham, *The Fiction of Frank Norris: The Aesthetic Context,* 42.
7. Compare Vandover's "boredom" aboard the Mazatlan. The narrator tells us that "Vandover had so accustomed himself to . . . self-indulgence that he could not go long with it. It had become a simple necessity for him to be amused" (381). But when we are told that Van "thought himself justified" in seeking amusement at this point "in order to forget about Ida's death" (381), another cause of this "simple necessity" becomes apparent. The need for amusement is one more reaction to loss.
8. Compare Mitchell, "Little Pictures," 390; Walter Benn Michaels, "The Gold Standard and the Logic of Naturalism," 105–32, *passim.*
9. Compare Miller, "The Art of Frank Norris in *Vandover*," 57.

10. Compare Graham, *Fiction of Frank Norris,* 36.
11. Ibid., 26.
12. Chapter XIV recapitulates the movement of the novel as a whole. It begins after Vandover has accepted the termination of his relationship with Turner and with the world to which she belongs. Vandover is at the opera; as he gives himself up to the music, it seems to him

> infinitely beautiful. . . . There came over him a vague sense of those things which are too beautiful to be comprehended, of a nobility, a self-oblivion, an immortal eternal love and kindness, . . . all joy for the true, the right and pure. . . . It was as if for the moment, he had become a little child again. (466–67)

For Vandover, the possibility of beauty, harmony, unity, value of any kind, necessarily involves a return to childhood. He becomes a "little child again" in a kind of prelapsarian universe, before the loss of his mother introduced discord, fear, and guilt into his world. Returning home from the opera, Vandover judges himself mercilessly for his failures and turns one last time to his art, seeking salvation. But by the end of Chapter XIV, his art, as Vandover sees it, has abandoned him too, destroying his tenuous, childlike sense of unity and possibility, recapitulating the experience that shattered the harmony of Vandover's actual childhood.
13. Vandover's idea that his art is "the one thing that could save him" (472) has in part been attributed to Vans naiveté (Graham, *Fiction of Frank Norris,* 17–18). Yet the idea is sporadically supported by the narrative voice without any discernible irony. In a passage such as the following, one cannot meaningfully differentiate between the narrative voice and Vandover's own state of mind:

> He had remembered his art, turning to it instinctively as he always did when greatly moved. It was the strongest side of him; it would be the last thing to go; he felt it there yet. It was the one thing that could save him. (472; compare 462, 481; compare William Dillingham, *Instinct and Art,* 12)

14. Compare Graham, *Fiction of Frank Norris,* 27; Miller, "The Art of Norris in *Vandover*," 62; Mitchell, "Little Pictures," 396–97.
15. The ending of *Vandover and the Brute* has not provoked as much comment as the endings of *McTeague* and *The Octopus*. Joseph McElrath has suggested, however, that the final scene of *Vandover* recalls Vandover's own childhood and is significant because childhood was the time of Van's moral indoctrination—the indoctrination with regard to the relation between reason and instinct that McElrath sees as "a prime cause of [Vandover's] psychic and physical degeneration" ("Frank Norris's *Vandover and the Brute,*" 184). Compare Miller, "The Art of Norris in *Vandover*," 62–63. Miller's essay, which considers *Vandover* from a psychoanalytic perspective, confirms my view that the death of Vandover's mother is a crucial event within Vandover's experience and within the novel as a whole. For earlier psychological readings of *Vandover,* see Maxwell Geismar's treatment of Vandover's "oedipal relationship" with his parents (*Rebels and Ancestors: The American Novel 1890–1915,* chap. 1) and Kenneth S. Lynn's "Frank Norris: Mama's Boy," in *The Dream of Success: A study of the Modern American Imagina-*

tion (158–208). Lynn's emphasis in his treatment of *Vandover* is Vandover's relationship with his father. For a different approach to the final scene, see Mitchell, "Little Pictures," 386–87, 404–5.
16. See Chapter 2. Compare Lee Clark Mitchell's emphasis on the coercive force of language in Vandover, "Little Pictures," 401, 405, and *passim*.
17. Compare Graham, *Fiction of Frank Norris,* 35; McElrath, "Frank Norris's *Vandover,"* 186–89; Stanley Cooperman, "Frank Norris and the Werewolf of Guilt," 257.
18. Compare Donald Pizer's reading of this scene in "The Problem of Philosophy in the Novel," 54–57; compare Graham, *Fiction of Frank Norris,* 2.

Notes to Chapter 4: Loss, Habit, Obsession: The Governing Dynamic of *McTeague*

1. See William B. Dillingham, "The Old Folks of *McTeague*," 347–48; George W. Johnson, "Frank Norris and Romance," 58; Donald Pizer, *The Novels of Frank Norris,* 57–58, 61–64, 69, 71.
2. See George M. Spangler, "The Structure of *McTeague*," 48 and *passim*; Edwin Haviland Miller, "The Art of Frank Norris in *McTeague*," 61–65; William Freedman, "Oral Passivity and Oral Sadism in Norris's *McTeague*," 52–61; compare Don Graham, "Art in *McTeague*" in *Critical Essays on Frank Norris,* 75–84; and Joseph H. Gardner, "Dickens, Romance and *McTeague*," 361–77.
3. Donald Pizer, "Another Look at *The Octopus*," 15.
4. Compare Gardner, "Dickens, Romance and *McTeague*," 376–77; Spangler, "The Structure of *McTeague*," 53.
5. Compare Gardner, "Dickens, Romance and *McTeague*," 376.
6. For a fine analysis of the Dickens connection in *McTeague,* see ibid., 367–68.
7. See William Dean Howells, "A Case in Point," in *Critical Essays on Frank Norris,* 15; compare Gardner, "Dickens, Romance and *McTeague*," 377; Joseph R. McElrath, Jr., "The Comedy of Frank Norris's *McTeague*," 94–95; Pizer, *The Novels of Frank Norris,* 74.
8. See Chapter 1.
9. Compare McTeague in Trina Sieppe's bedroom (57).
10. Two recent essays have noted the allusion to *Othello* in the line "Old Grannis's occupation was gone." See John Schroeder, "The Shakespearean Plots of *McTeague*," 294; compare William E. Cain, "Presence and Power in *McTeague*," 207–8.
11. See William B. Dillingham, *Frank Norris: Instinct and Art,* 74–75; Gardner, "Dickens, Romance and *McTeague*," 373–75; Charles Hoffman, "Norris and the Responsibility of the Novelist," 511; Pizer, *The Novels of Frank Norris,* 63, 69–70; Spangler, "The Structure of *McTeague*," 52–53.
12. Compare Gardner, "Dickens, Romance and *McTeague*," 373–75.
13. Compare Graham's argument that Trina is, on the contrary, more limited than McTeague (*The Fiction of Frank Norris: The Aesthetic Context,* 79–80).
14. For other discussions of the connection between Trina's greed and her sexuality, see Gardner, "Dickens, Romance and *McTeague*," 336, 339; Miller, "The Art of

Norris in *McTeague*," 64; Pizer, *The Novels of Frank Norris*, 70; Spangler, "The Structure of *McTeague*," 53.

15. Compare Graham, *Fiction of Frank Norris,* 79; Schroeder, "The Shakespearean Plots of *McTeague*," 293.

16. Compare Graham, *Fiction of Frank Norris,* 79; Miller, "The Art of Norris in *McTeague*," 62.

17. Problems of adaptation to change and loss are also central to the experience of the Sieppes and Marcus. For discussions of McTeague's "adaptability," see Johnson, "Frank Norris and Romance," 58–59; Freedman, "Oral Passivity in Norris's *McTeague*," 54; Pizer, *The Novels of Frank Norris,* 3, 62–64; compare Robert F. Sommer, "Norris's *McTeague*," 39–41.

Notes to Chapter 5: The Language of Recovery: Word and Symbol in *The Octopus*

1. William Dean Howells, "A Case in Point," 15.

2. Compare David Wyatt, "Norris and the Vertical," 758–59.

3. For some of the most important contributions to the debate over the philosophical and aesthetic coherence of *The Octopus,* see Richard Allen Davison, "Frank Norris's *The Octopus*," 103–5, 108, 111; William B. Dillingham, *Instinct and Art,* 63–65; Don Graham, *The Fiction of Frank Norris: The Aesthetic Context,* 119–22; Joseph R. McElrath, Jr., "Frank Norris's *The Octopus*," 140–48; George Wilbur Meyer, "A New Interpretation of *The Octopus*," 356, 358–59; Donald Pizer, *The Novels of Frank Norris,* 130–31, 135, 140–45; Robert Schneider, "Frank Norris: The Naturalist as Victorian," 21–23; William L. Vance, "Romance in *The Octopus*," 130, 132–34, and *passim.*

4. Criticism of *The Octopus* even shows a lack of consensus about who the "hero" of the novel is. While Marchand emphasizes the role of Magnus as "tragic" figure (*Frank Norris: A Study,* 148–49), Kenneth S. Lynn's long Introduction to *The Octopus,* as Vance points out, "does not so much as mention" Magnus. On the other hand, "Maxwell Geismar's lengthy discussion of the book . . . completely ignores Vanamee" (William L. Vance, "Romance in *The Octopus*," 135; compare Vance's own focus on what he takes to be the crucial role of Vanamee, 120–30). The majority of critics since the 1960s have tended to see Presley, Annixter, and Vanamee as the central figures of the novel, sometimes singling out one of these characters for special emphasis, but stressing the meaning of their experience in relation to one another, often in terms of their individual growth or "development." See Dillingham, *Instinct and Art,* 62–63; George W. Johnson, "Frank Norris and Romance," 62; Pizer, *The Novels of Frank Norris,* 125, 130–31, 136. Don Graham, for example, analyzes the nature of Presley's relation to aesthetic experience with Annixter and Vanamee serving as comparison and contrast. Compare Vance's view that the "parallelisms" in the portraits of Presley, Annixter, and Vanamee "are inadequate to 'bind the epic together'" ("Romance in *The Octopus*," 136 n. 12). Although Graham begins his discussion of *The Octopus* with the suggestion that Presley is "the most important single character" (68), he takes Annixter and Hilma "together

and separately" as the "heroes of the novel" (110). I agree with this assessment, though on different grounds.

5. It is not only at the end of the novel that Presley sees the wheat as irrepressible force (II, 360). Compare Presley's view of the wheat at the end of Book II, Chapter 4 (161); compare II, 286. For critical interpretations of the image of the wheat within the novel, see Davison, "Frank Norris's *The Octopus*," 109; Pizer, *The Novels of Frank Norris,* 127, 130, 133, 144–45, 156; Schneider, "Frank Norris: The Naturalist as Victorian," 23; compare Mark Seltzer, "The Naturalist Machine," 116–17, 128–29.

6. Compare James K. Folsom, "Social Darwinism or Social Protest? The 'Philosophy' of *The Octopus*," 397

7. The fact that the plot of *The Octopus* in effect "rewards" Vanamee for his single-mindedness remains, to my mind, the most serious flaw in the novel (compare Graham, *Fiction of Frank Norris,* 108). I will suggest that the textual evidence both within the Vanamee plot and in the surrounding context makes it impossible to see Vanamee's "victory" as a benign resolution. The problem of accounting for the logic of his final happiness remains, however. See Vance's discussion of the problematic nature of the Vanamee plot ("Romance in *The Octopus*," 120–30). Compare Davison, "Frank Norris's *The Octopus*," 107–9; Folsom, "Social Darwinism or Social Protest?," 395–97; McElrath, "Frank Norris's *The Octopus*," 139–40. A provocative contribution to the debate on Vanamee is John Jolly's article, "The Genesis of the Rapist in *The Octopus*." While Jolly's view of Vanamee himself as the rapist of Angèle is untenable (compare Glen Love, "Letter to the Editor," 149), his discussion of Vanamee is otherwise illuminating. Jolly's emphasis is Vanamee's need to "resume his development at the point in time when it ceased" (208) by trying to "alter history, at least in his [own] frame of reference" (201–2).

8. Compare Folsom, "Social Darwinism or Social Protest?," 397.

9. Presley's experience with his poem "The Toilers" provides another paradigm for the ambiguities of reality—of "art" as well as "life."

> Presley's Socialist poem, "The Toilers," had an enormous success. . . . It was promptly copied in New York, Boston and Chicago papers. It was discussed, attacked, defended, eulogized, ridiculed. It was praised with the most fulsome adulation, assailed with the most violent condemnation. (II, 108)

Poetry, in short, resists uniformity of interpretation, quite as much as nature.

10. A threat that elicits defensive behavior may be either external or internal and would seem to be the more devastating the more obscure or unspecific its source. An early scene between Harran and S. Behrman nicely confirms this point. Harran has come to the railroad station to meet his father and has noted with relief the presence of three flatcars loaded with the plows that he and his father have anxiously awaited. Harran's relief soon turns to fury, however, as S. Behrman reminds him of the "regulations" that make it mandatory for Eastern freight to "'go first to one of our common points and be reshipped from there.'"

> Harran did remember now, but never before had the matter so struck home. He leaned back in his seat in dumb amazement for the instant. Even Magnus had

> turned a little pale. Then, abruptly, Harran broke out, violent and raging.
>
> "What next? My God, why don't you break into our houses at night? Why don't you steal the watch out of my harness, hold us up with shotgun; yes, 'stand and deliver; your money or your life.'" (I, 67)

Although "the regulations" are public knowledge, Harran's rage springs from his sense of having been surprised by an undeclared enemy. His perspective is typical both within *The Octopus* and throughout Norris's work. An armed robber who states his aims and his terms, who indeed offers one a clear choice—your money or your life—is far preferable to an opponent like S. Behrman who never gets angry and who, unwilling to admit outright antagonism, can never be confronted.

11. It is striking to note in this context that Norris himself tended to use the same phrases—and sometimes the same paragraphs—in different works. To take an example from the present incident, the narrative voice says of Dyke that his "occupation [was] gone" (II, 72), echoing the line from *Othello* Norris had already used to describe Old Grannis in *McTeague.* On his way home from Bonneville in this episode, Dyke stops for a drink at Caraher's saloon, where his hands lie "open on the table before him, idle . . ." (II, 72), like those of both McTeague and Old Grannis at analogous points in their experiences (*McTeague,* 197, 236). Other examples abound, the most substantial involving *Blix, Vandover,* and Norris's Harvard themes. Compare James D. Hart, Introduction to *A Novelist in the Making,* 18–19, 21–22; Graham, *Fiction of Frank Norris,* 8–10.

12. Annixter is found reading *David Copperfield* for the last time shortly after his marriage. His thoughts wander, however, and no sooner is he said to be reading than he puts his book aside to consider the question of how to help Dyke's mother and daughter in their difficult time (II, 143). For a different account of Annixter's relationship to Hilma in terms of control and vulnerability, see Seltzer, "The Naturalist Machine," 127.

13. Compare Don Graham's reading of Presley's final conversation with Hilma (*Fiction of Frank Norris,* 121–22) and Pizer, *The Novels of Frank Norris,* 136. For a different perspective on the role of memory in *The Octopus,* see Wyatt, "Norris and the Vertical," 759–60.

14. Compare Percy Lubbock, *The Craft of Fiction* (29–33), and Edwin Muir's discussion of what he calls the "chronicle" and the framework of "universality" in *War and Peace* (*The Structure of the Novel,* 102–9, 112).

15. See Chapter 2.

16. Compare Benn Michaels, "Corporate Fiction," 192.

17. See Chapter 1. Norris rarely refers to the English romantic poets directly in either his work or his letters. Yet he read voraciously and clearly knew the work of Keats, Coleridge, and others. See, for example, Keats's "vale of Soul-making" letter (22 December 1817), especially the notion that a soul in possession of "the sense of Identity" may be formed through the integration of experience in time. In one instance, Norris mentions Keats briefly in a column from *The Critic* and goes on, shortly thereafter (without mentioning his source), to echo some phrases from Keats's "vale of Soul-Making" letter. Norris refers to the writer's "divine spark" that will be fanned, rather than extinguished, by the "breath of the millions" (209, 210;

compare Keats's "soul-making" letter, 277). In the same essay, moreover, Norris goes on to refer to a poem by Leigh Hunt, again without mentioning his source. Norris perhaps knew Keats's work more intimately than one can readily conclude from his lack of focus on the poet and his contemporaries.

Notes to Chapter 6: Coming of Age in *The Pit*

1. See Jesse S. Crisler and Joseph R. McElrath, Jr., *Frank Norris: A Reference Guide,* xi; Joseph R. McElrath, Jr., and Katherine Knight, *Frank Norris: The Critical Reception,* xvi-xvii; James D. Hart, *The Popular Book,* 220; Franklin Walker, *Frank Norris: A Biography,* 296.
2. Compare Richard Allen Davison, "A Reading of Frank Norris's *The Pit,*" 79; Joseph Katz, "Eroticism in American Literary Realism," 45–46; Howard Horwitz, "To Find the Value of X," 233; H. Wayne Morgan, "Frank Norris: The Romantic Naturalist," 142. See Charles Hoffman, "Norris and the Responsibility of the Novelist," 511, and William Dillingham, *Frank Norris: Instinct and Art,* 117—although both of these emphasize the wheat as such, rather than the Pit itself.
3. For consideration of the double plot, see Davison, "A Reading of *The Pit,*" 81–82, 94, and *passim*; Horwitz, "To Find the Value of X," 215–37; Ernst Marchand, *Frank Norris: A Study,* 86; Donald Pizer, *The Novels of Frank Norris,* 165, 174. For discussions of the ending, see Davison, "A Reading of *The Pit,*" 93–94; Don Graham, *The Fiction of Frank Norris: The Aesthetic Context,* 155; Horwitz, "To Find the Value of X," 232–34; Hoffman, "Norris and the Responsibility of the Novelist," 512–14; Larzer Ziff, *The American 1890's: Life and Times of a Lost Generation,* 273.
4. Here as elsewhere, Don Graham's work is invaluable. See his chapter on *The Pit* in *Fiction of Frank Norris.* Compare Katz, "Eroticism in Literary Realism" (46–48), and a master's thesis by Janie Helen Blitch, "*The Pit* and Allusive Revelations," which has been inaccessible to me. The most recent contribution to the growing picture of Norris's "allusive skill" is a revealing article by Mark L. Mitchell and Joseph R. McElrath, Jr., "Frank Norris's *The Pit*: Musical Elements as Biographical Evidence."
5. "The story is told through Laura Dearborn," Norris wrote to Isaac Marcosson in November 1901: "[S]he occupies the center of the stage all the time, and I shall try to interest the reader more in the problems of her character and career than in any other human element in the book" ("Ten Letters by Frank Norris," 59–60).
6. Laura often speaks of her "being" as a fragmented, unknown, and perhaps unknowable entity. "'I hope I won't come to myself some day, after it is too late, and find that it was all a mistake,'" Laura tells Mrs. Cressler after announcing her intention to marry Jadwin. "'You don't know how nervous I am these days. One minute I am one kind of girl, and the next another kind. . . . I don't know myself these days'" (162–63). Laura never arrives at a moment where the notion of "self" acquires stable form and meaning. Instead, for Laura, experience is more often than not "a whirl, a blur [within which . . . s]he had not been able to find herself" (205; compare 396). Laura repeatedly expresses the sense of being "two" even "three" Lauras (251, 405). Despite brief periods of relative stability (see 205), she remains subject to

rapidly changing moods in which she "no longer knew herself" (291) and within which she becomes aware of "depths in her nature she had not plumbed . . . hidden pitfalls" of which she is "afraid" (359).

7. For an impressive analysis relating the first scene in *Faust* to Laura's "seduction" by Corthell, see Katz, "Eroticism in Literary Realism," 44–49.

8. Compare McTeague and Old Grannis in *McTeague*; Dyke in *The Octopus*; and Ferriss in *A Man's Woman,* where amputated hands are the forerunners of death. The *Othello* connection we have noted in the line "Old Grannis's occupation was gone" receives additional emphasis in the context of *The Pit,* with its focus on the coherence of the self as well as the issues of both jealousy and drama. See Chapters 1 and 4.

9. Compare Graham, *Fiction of Frank Norris,* 149.

10. Compare Katz, "Eroticism in Literary Realism," 48.

11. Compare Davison, "A Reading of *The Pit,*" 87–88.

12. See Chapter 2. Compare the static paradise of the Old Folks in *McTeague.*

13. This view of Creation also recalls the Archangels' opening speeches in the "Prolog Im Himmel" of *Faust* (lines 243–70).

14. *Faust,* too, of course begins with a "bargain" that has crucial implications for the structure of the text it introduces.

15. See Roland Barthes, *The Pleasure of the Text,* 47; Peter Brooks, *Reading for the Plot,* 64; compare Janice Doane and Devon Hodges, *Nostalgia and Sexual Difference,* 71–72.

16. In his article on *The Pit,* Richard Allen Davison is one of the few critics besides Don Graham who gives serious attention to the figure of Page ("A Reading of *The Pit,*" 81–82).

17. Compare Mitchell and McElrath, "Musical Elements," 165–73.

18. "'What's the fool talking about?'" Jadwin exclaims when Laura tries introducing him to "her beloved Meredith" (215). Predictably, Jadwin's favorite writer is Howells, especially his *The Rise of Silas Lapham.* "I'm not long very many of art," Jadwin says, "[b]ut I believe that any art that don't make the world better and happier is no art at all, and is only fit for the dump heap" (216).

19. Compare Davison, "A Reading of *The Pit,*" 82.

Notes to Afterword: A Parting Glance

1. We know that Norris was reading Henry James around this time. See *The Letters of Frank Norris,* 72; compare Davison, "A Reading of Frank Norris's *The Pit,*" 89.

Works Cited

Åhnebrink, Lars. *The Beginnings of Naturalism in American Fiction.* Upsala and Cambridge: A. B. Lundequistska Bokhandeln and Harvard University Press, 1950.

Barthes, Roland. *The Pleasure of the Text.* Translated by Richard Miller. New York: Hill and Wang, 1975.

Biencourt, Marius. *Une influence du naturalisme français en Amérique: Frank Norris.* Paris: Giard, 1933.

Brooks, Peter. *Reading for the Plot.* New York: Vintage Books, 1985.

Blitch, Janie Helen. "*The Pit* and Allusive Revelations." M.A. thesis, University of Texas, 1970.

Cain, William E. "Presence and Power in *McTeague.*" In *American Realism,* edited by Eric J. Sundquist. Baltimore: Johns Hopkins University Press, 1982.

Coleridge, Samuel Taylor. "The Rime of the Ancient Mariner" and "Kubla Khan." In *Coleridge: Poetry and Prose,* edited by Carlos Baker. New York: Bantam, 1965.

Cooper, Frederic Taber. *Some American Storytellers.* New York: Henry Holt, 1911.

Cooperman, Stanley. "Frank Norris and the Werewolf of Guilt." *Modern Language Quarterly* 20 (1959): 252–58.

Crisler, Jesse S., and Joseph R. McElrath, Jr. *Frank Norris: A Reference Guide.* Boston: G. K. Hall, 1974.

Crow, Charles L. "The Real Vanamee and His Influence on Frank Norris's *The Octopus.*" *Western American Literature* 9 (1974): 131–39.

Davison, Richard Allen. "Frank Norris's *The Octopus*: Some Observations on Vanamee, Shelgrim and St. Paul." In *Critical Essays on Frank Norris,* edited by Don Graham, 99–115. Boston: G. K. Hall.

———. "A Reading of Frank Norris's *The Pit.*" In *The Stoic Strain in American Literature,* edited by Duane J. MacMillan, 77–94. Toronto: University of Toronto Press, 1979.

Dillingham, William B. "Frank Norris and the Genteel Tradition." In *Critical Essays on Frank Norris,* edited by Don Graham, 194–204. Boston: G. K. Hall. 1980.

———. *Frank Norris: Instinct and Art.* Lincoln: University of Nebraska Press, 1969.

———. "The Old Folks of *McTeague.*" In *McTeague,* edited by Donald Pizer, 344–48. New York: W. W. Norton & Co., 1977.

Doane, Janice, and Devon Hodges. *Nostalgia and Sexual Difference*. New York and London: Methuen, 1987.

Folsom, James K. "Social Darwinism or Social Protest? The 'Philosophy' of *The Octopus*." *Modern Fiction Studies* 8 (1962): 393–400.

Freedman, William. "Oral Passivity and Oral Sadism in Norris's *McTeague*." *Literature and Psychology* 30 (1980): 52–61.

French, Warren G. *Frank Norris*. New York: Twayne Publishers, 1962.

Gardner, Joseph H. "Dickens, Romance and *McTeague*: A Study in Mutual Interpretation." In *McTeague,* edited by Donald Pizer, 361–77. New York: W. W. Norton & Co., 1977.

Geismar, Maxwell. *Rebels and Ancestors: The American Novel 1890–1915*. New York: Hill and Wang, 1963.

Goethe, Wolfgang von. *Faust.* Edited by Erich Trunz. Hamburg: Christian Wegner Verlag, 1963.

Goldsmith, Arnold L. "The Development of Frank Norris's Philosophy." In *Studies in Honor of John Wilcox,* edited by Woodburn O. Ross and A. Dayle Wallace, 175–94. Detroit: Wayne State University Press, 1957.

Graham, Don. *The Fiction of Frank Norris: The Aesthetic Context.* Columbia: University of Missouri Press, 1978.

Graham, Don, ed. *Critical Essays on Frank Norris.* Boston: G. K. Hall, 1980.

Hart, James D. Introduction to *A Novelist in the Making*. Cambridge: Harvard University Press, 1970.

———. *The Popular Book.* New York: Oxford University Press, 1950.

Hochman, Baruch. "On the Imagination of Death." *Denver Quarterly* 10 (1975): 30–49.

Hoffman, Charles. "Norris and the Responsibility of the Novelist." *The South Atlantic Quarterly* 54 (1955): 509–14.

Horwitz, Howard. "To Find the Value of X: *The Pit* as a Renunciation of Romance." In *American Realism,* edited by Eric J. Sundquist. Baltimore: Johns Hopkins University Press, 1982.

Howells, William Dean. "A Case in Point." In *Critical Essays on Frank Norris,* edited by Don Graham, 13–15. Boston: G. K. Hall, 1980.

Johnson, George W. "Frank Norris and Romance." *American Literature* 33 (1961): 52–63.

Jolly, John. "The Genesis of the Rapist in *The Octopus*." *Western American Literature* 17 (1982): 201–12.

Katz, Joseph. "Eroticism in American Literary Realism." *Studies in American Fiction* 5 (1977): 35–50.

Kazin, Alfred. *On Native Grounds*. New York: Harcourt Brace Jovanovich, 1942.

Keats, John. "Ode on a Grecian Urn," "Ode to a Nightingale," "Letters." In *Complete Poetical Works*. Boston: Houghton Mifflin, 1890.

Kipling, Rudyard. "Her Majesty's Servants." In *The Jungle Book,* vol. 2. Garden City, N.Y.: Doubleday, 1948.
Lawlor, Mary. "'Life' and 'Literature' in Frank Norris's Cowboy Tales." *Prairie Winds* (Spring-Summer 1986): 34–40.
Love, Glen. "Letter to the Editor." *Western American Literature* 18 (1983): 149.
Lubbock, Percy. *The Craft of Fiction.* New York: Peter Smith, 1947.
Lynn, Kenneth. *The Dream of Success: A Study of the Modern American Imagination.* Boston: Little, Brown, 1955.
———. Introduction to *The Octopus.* Boston: Houghton Mifflin, 1959.
McElrath, Joseph R., Jr. "The Comedy of Frank Norris's *McTeague.*" *Studies in American Humor* 2 (1975): 88–95.
———. "The Erratic Design of Frank Norris's *Moran of the Lady Letty.*" *American Literary Realism* 10 (1977): 114–24.
———. "Frank Norris: A Biographical Essay." *American Literary Realism* 11 (1978): 219–34.
———. "Frank Norris: Early Posthumous Responses." *American Literary Realism* 12 (1979): 1–76.
———. "Frank Norris's *The Octopus*: The Christian Ethic as Pragmatic Response." In *Critical Essays on Frank Norris,* edited by Don Graham, 138–52. Boston: G. K. Hall, 1980.
———. "Frank Norris's *Vandover and the Brute*: Narrative Technique and the Socio-Critical Viewpoint." *Studies in American Fiction* 4 (1976): 27–45.
McElrath, Joseph R., Jr., and Katherine Knight. *Frank Norris: The Critical Reception.* New York: B. Franklin, 1979.
Marchand, Ernst. *Frank Norris: A Study.* Stanford, Calif.: Stanford University Press, 1942.
Meyer, George Wilbur. "A New Interpretation of *The Octopus.*" *College English* 4 (1943): 351–59.
Michaels, Walter Benn. "Corporate Fiction: Norris, Royce, and Arthur Machen." In *Reconstructing American Literary History,* edited by Sacvan Berkovitch, 189–219. Cambridge and London: Harvard University Press, 1986.
———. "The Gold Standard and the Logic of Naturalism." *Representations* 9 (1985): 105–32.
Miller, Edwin Haviland. "The Art of Frank Norris in *McTeague.*" *The Markham Review* 8 (1979): 61–5.
———. "The Art of Frank Norris in *Vandover and the Brute.*" *The Markham Review* 10 (1981): 56–63.
Mitchell, Lee Clark. "Little Pictures on the Lacquered Surface: The Determining Vocabularies of Norris's *Vandover and the Brute.*" *Papers on Language and Literature* 22 (1986): 386–405.
Mitchell, Mark L., and Joseph R. McElrath, Jr. "Frank Norris's *The Pit*:

Musical Elements as Biographical Evidence." *Papers on Language and Literature* 23 (1987): 161–74.

Morgan, H. Wayne. "Frank Norris: The Romantic as Naturalist." In *American Writers in Rebellion from Mark Twain to Dreiser.* New York: Hill & Wang, 1965.

Muir, Edwin. *The Structure of the Novel.* London: Hogarth Press, 1974.

Munn, Debra, D. "The Revision of Frank Norris's *Blix.*" *Resources for American Literary Study* 10 (1980): 47–55.

Norris, Charles. *Frank Norris.* New York: Doubleday, 1914.

Norris, Frank. *Blix.* In *A Novelist in the Making,* edited by James D. Hart. Cambridge: Harvard University Press, 1970.

———. *Critic* 40 (June 1902): 200–208. In *The Literary Criticism of Frank Norris,* edited by Donald Pizer. New York: Russell and Russell, 1964.

———. "Frank Norris's Weekly Letter." In *The Literary Criticism of Frank Norris,* edited by Donald Pizer. New York: Russell and Russell, 1964.

———. "His Sister." In *Frank Norris of "The Wave,"* 33–42. San Francisco: Westgate Press, 1931.

———. "The Jongleur of Taillebois." *The Complete Edition of Frank Norris,* 10:3–20. New York: Doubleday.

———. "Lauth." *The Complete Edition of Frank Norris,* 10:115–47. New York: Doubleday, 1928.

———. *The Letters of Frank Norris.* Edited by Franklin Walker. San Francisco: Book Club of California, 1956.

———. *McTeague.* New York: Holt, Rinehart & Winston, 1968.

———. *A Man's Woman.* New York: AMS Press, 1970. (Reprint of the 1931 edition.)

———. *Moran of the Lady Letty. The Complete Edition of Frank Norris,* vol. 3. New York: Doubleday, 1928.

———. "The Novel with a Purpose." In *The Literary Criticism of Frank Norris,* edited by Donald Pizer. New York: Russell and Russell, 1964.

———. "Novelists of the Future: The Training They Need." In *The Literary Criticism of Frank Norris,* edited by Donald Pizer. New York: Russell and Russell, 1964.

———. "Novelists to Order—While You Wait." In *The Literary Criticism of Frank Norris,* edited by Donald Pizer. New York: Russell and Russell, 1964.

———. "An Opening for Novelists: Great Opportunities for Fiction Writers in San Francisco." In *The Literary Criticism of Frank Norris,* edited by Donald Pizer. New York: Russell and Russell, 1964.

———. *The Octopus.* New York: Doubleday, 1901.

———. *The Pit.* New York: Doubleday, 1903.

———. "A Plea for Romantic Fiction." In *The Literary Criticism of Frank Norris,* edited by Donald Pizer. New York: Russell and Russell, 1964.

———. "A Problem in Fiction: Truth vs. Accuracy." In *The Literary Criticism of Frank Norris,* edited by Donald Pizer. New York: Russell and Russell, 1964.

———. "The Puppets and the Puppy: A Dialogue." In *Frank Norris of "The Wave,"* 175–80. San Francisco: Westgate Press, 1931.

———. "The Remaining Seven of Frank Norris's Weekly Letters." Edited by Richard Allen Davison. *American Literary Realism* 3 (1968): 47–65.

———. "Storytellers vs. Novelists." In *The Literary Criticism of Frank Norris,* edited by Donald Pizer. New York: Russell and Russell, 1964.

———. "Ten Letters by Frank Norris." Edited by Donald Pizer. *Book Club of California Quarterly News-Letter* 27 (1962): 51–61.

———. *Vandover and the Brute.* In *A Novelist in the Making,* edited by James D. Hart. Cambridge: Harvard University Press, 1970.

———. "Yvernelle." *The Complete Edition of Frank Norris,* vol. 6. New York: Doubleday, 1928.

———. "Zola as a Romantic Writer." In *The Literary Criticism of Frank Norris,* edited by Donald Pizer. New York: Russell and Russell, 1964.

Pizer, Donald. "Another Look at *The Octopus*." *Nineteenth Century Fiction* 10 (1955): 217–24.

———. "The Concept of Nature in Frank Norris's *The Octopus*." *American Quarterly* 14 (1962): 73–80.

———. *The Novels of Frank Norris.* Bloomington: Indiana University Press, 1966.

———. "The Problem of Philosophy in the Novel." *Bucknell Review* 18 (1970): 53–62.

———. *Realism and Naturalism in Nineteenth Century American Literature.* Carbondale and Edwardsville: Southern Illinois University Press, 1966.

Pizer, Donald, ed. *The Literary Criticism of Frank Norris.* New York: Russell and Russell. 1964.

———. *McTeague.* New York: W. W. Norton and Co., 1977.

Schneider, Robert W. "Frank Norris: The Naturalist as Victorian." *Midcontinent American Studies Journal* 3 (1964): 13–27.

Schroeder, John. "The Shakespearean Plots of *McTeague*." *American Literary Realism* 14 (1981): 289–96.

Seltzer, Mark. "The Naturalist Machine." In *Sex, Politics, and Science in the Nineteenth-Century Novel.* Baltimore: Johns Hopkins University Press, 1986.

Shakespeare, William. *Othello.* New York: Cambridge University Press, 1976.

———. *The Tempest.* New York: Cambridge University Press, 1976.

Sommer, Robert F. "Norris's *McTeague*." *The Explicator* 4 (1982): 39–41.

Spangler, George M. "The Structure of *McTeague*." *English Studies* 59 (1978): 48–56.

Tsur, Reuven. "Two Critical Attitudes: Quest for Certitude and Negative Capability." *College English* 36 (1975): 776–88.
Vance, William L. "Romance in *The Octopus*." In *Critical Essays on Frank Norris,* edited by Don Graham. Boston: G. K. Hall, 1980.
Walcutt, Charles Child. *American Literary Naturalism: A Divided Stream.* Minneapolis: University of Minnesota Press, 1956.
Walker, Franklin, *Frank Norris: A Biography.* New York: Russell and Russell, 1963.
Wyatt, David, "Norris and the Vertical." *The Southern Review* 19 (1983): 749–64.
Ziff, Larzer. *The American 1890's: Life and Times of a Lost Generation.* New York: Viking Press, 1966.

Index